Praise for *Air Mail*

"*Air Ma* end-
ship forged nidst
of the cor s are
pure outpo life,
sent back a ivide,
missives 'as necessary as air, beautiful and maternal and brutal all at once.' Houston and Irvine
reveal the ferocity of women who have made their
lives in the wilderness and by the pen, the depths
of wisdom hard-won, survival and what it cost,
and all of this in a language where horse hooves
can be heard thundering. They invite us to read
our precarious moment in the light of conscience,
as they excavate the layers of denial and historical
amnesia that have kept us from knowing who we
are, and then with determination and grace, they
envision our possible future."

—CAROLYN FORCHÉ, author of *In the
Lateness of the World*

"This epistolary exchange, which becomes a
friendship, and then a fierce and loving sistership,
reminds us that solidarity, by which maybe I really
mean *love*, emerges in conversation—in listening,
in asking, in sharing, in wondering, in sorrowing,
in raging, in attempting, in *dreaming*. In dreaming
together, with each other, and for each other. This
takes practice, and it takes care. Pam Houston and
Amy Irvine's *Air Mail* is evidence of that practice.
It is evidence, and a seed, of that care."

—ROSS GAY, author of *The Book of Delights*

"What happens when two brilliant women write to each other across the time and space of our present tense? Nothing short of a secular miracle, that's what. These epistolary love notes between Pam Houston and Amy Irvine bring rivers and mountains and valleys onto the page and into your heart, reminding you how you are still part of a body that matters. They bring hope and imagination wide as the sky. They bring the beauty of animals and trees, the hum of motherhood drumming up from the very ground, the hard truths and difficult days of violence and virus woven through with what's left in us: fight, resilience, and astonishingly, song. This is your present tense calling you to action out of the mouth of despair. This book is fierce love in motion, which is to say, everything worth anything on the planet begins intimately."

—LIDIA YUKNAVITCH, author of *Verge*

"As these two new 'old' friends discuss their hopes and fears I find myself nodding or taking a deep breath or saying 'Yes!' as their shared experiences mirror some of my own. This collection of letters will serve as a longstanding reminder of where we are and where we hope to end up in the future."

—ANNE HOLMAN, The King's English Bookshop

AIR MAIL

AIR MAIL

Letters of Politics, Pandemics, and Place

PAM HOUSTON   AMY IRVINE

Illustrations by
Claire Taylor

TORREY HOUSE PRESS

SALT LAKE CITY • TORREY

Versions of some of the following letters initially appeared in *Orion* Magazine.

First Torrey House Press Edition, October 2020
Copyright © 2020 by Pam Houston and Amy Irvine

Published by Torrey House Press
Salt Lake City, Utah
www.torreyhouse.org

International Standard Book Number: 978-1-948814-38-6
E-book ISBN: 978-1-948814-39-3
Library of Congress Control Number: 2020938536

Cover art by Claire Taylor
Interior art by Claire Taylor
Cover design by Kathleen Metcalf
Interior design by Rachel Buck-Cockayne
Distributed to the trade by Consortium Book Sales and Distribution

Torrey House Press offices in Salt Lake City sit on homelands of Ute, Goshute, Shoshone, and Paiute nations. Offices in Torrey are in homelands of Paiute, Ute, and Navajo nations.

For Natalie Maines, who wouldn't just shut up and sing, and for CHICKS, everywhere.

Dear reader,

When we began writing letters to each other in March of 2020, shortly after the COVID-19 outbreak led to Colorado's governor issuing a state-wide stay-at-home order, we had never met, and only knew each other through the books we had written. These books were all, in one way or another, about how the Earth's wild places saved us, raised us, mothered us, and brought us back to life. We live on opposite sides of the Continental Divide, on opposite sides of the San Juan Mountain Range. The rain that falls onto Pam's high mountain meadow will make its way eventually to the Atlantic Ocean, while the rain that falls onto Amy's high desert mesa will run toward the Pacific. The land between our houses, much of it over ten thousand feet in elevation, is arguably the most beautiful and wildest country in the lower 48.

In a culture defined by Twitter and the twenty-four-hour news cycle, writing letters felt like ritual—intimate, ancient—two barn owls calling to each other across a starry sky. As the reality of COVID set in, our letters became a life raft of clarity in days filled with increasing numbers of the dead and the incessant dismantling of our government from within. In them, we could rage and cry, hold each other up, and talk ourselves back into agency, back into hope, back into action. We could hear each other's voices and our own, ringing like bells, reminding us that the fight to save the Earth is what we were born for. Eventually we could hear your voice too, dear reader, your fear for the future, and your passion for the land.

Our voices are just part of a broader resistance. These letters were already assembled for publication and in the final proofreading stage when George Floyd was murdered and protests against police brutality and systemic racism flared across the nation—a long-overdue mass exercise in First Amendment rights that has been met with violence while those flexing Second Amendment muscle by storming state capitals armed with assault weapons have been met with zero pushback. We acknowledge that whatever threats COVID and distruction of the planet pose to us, to the very basic right to draw a full, clean, and healthy breath, those threats are at least tenfold to Black, Brown, and Indigenous people. Whatever fear and outrage we carry as our own, we hold far more of it for those more likely to die at the hands of law enforcement, in their jobs as essential workers, in their communities more polluted and underserved.

Dear Reader, you are the one we've been waiting for. We've caught up to a future we could not imagine, but we've known all along we were ready.

We'll see you soon, in the sky.

Amy and Pam

Hi Amy,

Greetings from the east-facing side of the Great Divide!

One of the things you and I have in common during this pandemic is that unlike most Americans who are sheltering in place, we have unrestricted access to vast parcels of the natural world right out our door. If I step down off my back porch and hop my fence, I am in the Rio Grande National Forest. If I keep walking, in a few hours I'll enter the Weminuche Wilderness, and after a couple days I'll get to the San Juan National Forest (four million acres altogether). I can wander around for weeks up there—especially now that the tourists have been discouraged—without seeing another soul. In this way we are the opposite of those Italians singing from their balconies.

We chose these lives. We were lucky and worked hard and cashed in our white middle-class privilege precisely so we would have unrestricted access to wild country, and even COVID, which is threatening to shut down the entire world, won't keep us out. An amazement, really, as I watch all the parks, state and national, around the country, closing. We can't go to a restaurant or to Paris, but we can still lose ourselves in the wilderness we love.

I've been thinking about the wildlands that get more use than ours, that grapple with a constant onslaught of people, and are suddenly emptied of them. I picture the animals whispering to one another, *Do you think they are all dead down there?* Then I picture them linking arms and dancing around the campfire. I hear the trees bending towards one another and singing. You might have seen the article in *Forbes* with the headline, "Coronavirus Lockdown Likely Saved 77,000 Lives in China Just by the Reduction of Air Pollution."

For all the suffering, heartache, grief, and economic catastrophe this virus will cause, I can't help but wonder what reevaluation of our priorities might come out of it. Will we learn we don't need so many choices? Will we get better at being, instead of doing? Will we remember that we *are* actually nature, and neither its master, nor the beneficiary of its charms? Will clean air, just as one example, seem like a thing worth staying home for?

Be well,
       Pam

Good morning Pam,

Hailing from the other side of the divide! I live off-grid on a remote mesa that connects the fourteen-thousand-foot peaks of Colorado's San Juan Mountains with the redrock deserts of my Utah homeland. In every direction there are millions of acres of public forests, canyons, basin and range. A quick morning walk in a shallow, unremarkable gully might reveal a mountain lion and her two teenagers, playing on the hillside, just fifty yards away. A scramble through jumbled boulders might prompt a spotted owl to rush out at you, to graze your head and send you reeling—the scrapes and bruises well worth the price of admission. The day Devin and I decided to marry, we were walking a stone's throw from the house when, in the dirt and duff, two matching arrowheads made themselves known.

Like many writers, I believed that something akin to Thoreau's life at Walden was necessary for both craft and soul. Not an hour goes by that I'm not brought to my knees by the lands I live next

7

to—the beauty, the freedom, and the promise that the natural world will go on, despite our species' appetites and expansions. Since our shared governor issued a statewide stay-at-home order, I've been more grateful than ever for this wide-open space to wander in, to be in relationship with. At the same time, I am aware that if this life is necessary for stories that connect us to the natural world, we will lose storytellers as quickly as we're losing people to this new virus. This life of ours cannot be the prerequisite.

You ask, as public life contracts, if we might realize we need not so many choices. One hopes. What if one doesn't have the luxury of choosing to live and write where and how we do? What if one has but a single patch of sky that she sees out a tiny, smog-smeared factory window?

If it's the patch of sky in China, it's a big fucking deal. For the first time in a long while, tens of thousands of Chinese citizens can take a breath and not worry that the pollution will kill them. For the first time in many of their children's lives, they are seeing the sky is *blue*. We've taken these things for granted. Let's hope we get to take them for granted in the future, by no longer taking them for granted here and now.

I'm also curious to hear you say more about "being" vs "doing." That seems like a major reset for America. How do you think we might manage this shift?

So glad to be in conversation,
                              Amy

Hi Amy,

We just got back from a hike in a canyon called Embargo Creek. It was meant to be eight miles round trip, but my younger wolfhound, Henry, let the snowmelt and the springtime smells put him into his wild mind and he climbed a ridge that dropped him down into another drainage (following not elk, not deer, but only the smells they left behind) and it took us a couple of extra hours to be reunited. The bluebirds were out in force and we scared up an annoyed coyote, watched a red-tail soar.

I was thinking about our conversation, and how lucky we are to get the thing we need most during lockdown, but also thinking there are many people, some of my dearest friends in fact, who would trade the day I just had for an hour in their favorite coffee shop with a macchiato and a morning bun, or a Wilco concert, or a baseball game. I have picked, intentionally, three things I love too, but I don't need them the way I need my boots on hard ground. And it's a good thing for the land, that it's not everybody's first choice. As you have written about so powerfully in *Desert Cabal*, the land has more of us out there loving it than it can stand.

I don't *know* how you get from living in a fast-paced city full of art and technology to loving the wilderness enough to write powerfully about it, though we both know great writers who do. I am so driven by my senses, my hands-and-feet-on experience of the physical stuff of landscape that it's almost impossible for me to imagine finding those drivers without days and weeks outside. But I could hope to channel whatever Leslie Marmon Silko found when she was missing the mesas of the Laguna Pueblo so fiercely, the exquisite novel *Ceremony* emerged.

I also have noticed that fewer and fewer of my students, especially at UC Davis, take a real interest in the natural world, fewer of them go backpacking, fewer of them could even define the nouns that have always made my heart beat fast: elk, mesa, trilobite, eddy.

There is no reason the one percent in China need to eat domestically raised wild pangolin at their cocktail parties. There is no reason the one percent in America needed to have their billions tripled in the months we ought to have been testing for this virus and preventing some, maybe a lot, of the carnage we are about to see. Maybe those Chinese children will see the blue sky and decide they like it that way. I know this sounds impossibly naive, but I do believe that is how the world changes.

My dirty little secret is I fly on too many airplanes. And I like it—have liked it all my life. I love to go, to see what I have not seen before. The places I teach around the country and the world have become like second homes: Sitka, Provincetown, Chamonix. As my awareness about the climate catastrophe has grown exponentially over the last decade, I've known I had to address my airplane problem. Which is related to my "doing" problem. I say yes to every job, every talk, every teaching opportunity. I make a Tetris game out of my schedule and I squeeze additional events in on twelve-hour layovers, and when my schedule is so full I hardly breathe or sleep; that is when I'm sure I am earning my place here. I have barely been home at all in the eighteen months since *Deep Creek* was published because I have been so busy proving proving proving I am worthy—until now. It is the sickest thing about me, this workaholism, and I don't know when or if I would have ever slowed down, if this virus hadn't forced me to. In a way I am like those Chinese children. If I don't die from

COVID, COVID might end up adding years to my life.

So now I am *being*, or at least something closer to it. Every day, a multi-hour walk with the dogs, every day a bath. I cook luxuriously complicated soups and stews. I work. I am overseeing nine graduate student theses at two universities, so there is always reading and critiquing. I am writing, a little. That may sound like plenty of doing, but the difference is I am not chasing anything. For the first time in a long time, I am just here.

I know you teach as well, and I am curious what changes you see in your students' relationship to the natural world, and how much influence you think any mentor can have. In *Desert Cabal* you said we needed to come together to love the wilderness more gently, and sometimes from a respectful distance, to raise our voices in unison to save what is left of it. How do you communicate that to the young people you work with?

Take care,
Pam

Dear Pam,

First off, I am so glad you found your dog!

It's noon and I'm just sitting down to my desk. There were a neighbor's chickens to stock in the pot (I'm freezing a bunch of broth; my Mormon prepper genes just love a good apocalypse). Then I made pumpkin muffins, thinking my daughter would love waking up to them. But instead Ruby woke up frozen in trauma. Medical trauma related to her two autoimmune disorders. So there was time spent talking her down, back into her body.

One of the things I love about Victorian novels is how letter-writing forges such bonds between two people. In the urgent age of LOLs and heart emojis, I knew I missed that more personal kind of back and forth—but in the age of COVID-19, I find it as vital as being out on the land. I count this conversation as one of the gifts to come out of this pandemic. One gain amid so much loss.

Other meaningful correspondence this week: Leslie Jamison, who just published a gripping essay about being quarantined in Brooklyn, alone with a toddler and the coronavirus. She's on the mend, thank god, but her experience is so different from ours. There's Nadia Owusu, who would love to live next to the western wilds with us but who knows it's not the easiest or safest place for a Black woman to be. Regina Lopez-Whiteskunk, a member of the Ute Mountain Ute Tribe, who is trying to shine some light on how the virus will wallop nearby Indigenous communities that were already underserved. My mother, who is holed up in Salt Lake City, where an earthquake and hundreds of aftershocks reminds me that the planet is trying to shrug us off in more ways than one. Ditto for Lydia Peelle, who is navigating this new normal in the ruin of her Nashville neighborhood, thanks to the tornado that tore through on Super Tuesday. My god, that day seems like a year ago.

I acknowledge these women, their circumstances, because I am so kinetically aware of the contrast between our lives and theirs. Each of them deeply loves the natural world and is wrought over what's happening to it. But with the exception of Regina—whose life remains rooted in her desert homeland—I think the other three might choose the macchiato, or the concert (maybe not the baseball game!).

Leslie, Nadia, and Lydia are examples of

women writing about the natural world, about threats to it, even as they live in big cities and do big-city things. But their writing cannot be pegged as "nature writing." Which is a good thing. I'm not sure that those of us whose books end up on that shelf are changing public consciousness or policy as much as we'd like to think we are; we're often just preaching to the choir. I am grateful to my friends who are writing about all things perilous to the planet in a broader way, in stories intended for a broader readership. Your books, Pam, achieve that. I've assigned your memoir, *Deep Creek*, to some of my nonfiction students—women who have never stepped foot into a wilderness area and likely never will. It's such a big-hearted story, and it prompted these students to scan the perimeter of their own lives, to examine how they were shaped by place.

Back to Leslie, Nadia and Lydia, to name just three: they may not be out on the land all the time, but they very much care about oceans rising and climate refugees. They are no less heartbroken than we are that starving orcas are preying on great white sharks because there's so few fish left in the sea. They are no less furious that yesterday the EPA announced that industry could pollute our air, water, and bodies to their ice-cold hearts' delight.

Which reminds me: this year is the fiftieth anniversary of the Clean Air Act—or what's left of it.

The MFA program I teach in is a low-residency program, so many of my students already have families and careers. It's all they can do to finish up their day job and tend to family, chores. It's hard for them to view creative writing as something *not* to be squeezed in the way some folks cram in a spin class. Not that I fault them; most days I'm hard-pressed for five minutes on the balcony at sunset. But if I don't claw my way back into the carnality of my life, I might as well be another casualty of this new virus.

I try to teach embodiment with that kind of urgency. I have students stand in a scene that they've written. We reconstruct the angle of light, the warped floorboard, the stroke of willow branches on the window. I direct other students to step in—not only as other human characters, but also as key elements of the story: The window frame. The tree. If they can just linger, the sensual opens them to the emotional. Often, students jump out of their bodies, retreat back into their heads. I bring them back, help them stay with that level of physical and emotional intensity. I tell them it's a bit like climbing at altitude—you ascend in increments, to acclimatize.

To endure trauma, however, it's vital to leave the body. As was the case with my daughter this morning—she's been subjected to so many tests, drugs, and procedures—so the goal was to re-embody. To feel and speak about the lived experience, so that she could move beyond the tyranny of that memory.

If we are anything in this new reality, we are collectively traumatized—and therefore tyrannized—first by the climate crisis, and now by the novel coronavirus. But these traumas won't affect us equally. Black and brown people will suffer far worse than white people. Even those of us who don't view ourselves as racist will still make choices that further jeopardize the less fortunate. Like you, the choice I struggle with is airplane travel—not only do I love the adventure, it's been integral to how I make a living. We go where we must, physically and psychically, to find the story. I machete the carbon everywhere else, as compensation.

This leads me to the thing I most want to ask you, to ask all the poets and writers I admire: How does this pandemic, the stay-at-home life it demands, change what you are writing? What sort of stories do we tell now?

Wishing you wellness,
Amy

Hi Amy,

Well, I am not Mormon, but I am a good old-fashioned Utah river guide and I can manage a 120-quart Gott cooler and all the food inside it into meals that allow not one single thing to go bad during a twenty-one-day river trip. My nickname on the river was "Oh Great Protectress of the Block Ice." We all have our special skills to bring to bear.

Letters *are* a good thing we have largely lost, though my friend Fenton Johnson writes them still, meaning he never took a break, and it is one reason I think our friendship has stayed so dear across the years and miles. You and I would not be learning about each other in this particular way without this pandemic, nor about ourselves. And speaking of miles, I mapped our distance from one another just now and we are four hours and 209 miles apart as the car drives, 119 miles and forty-one hours apart as the hiking boots walk. Elevation gained and lost during those forty-one hours? Undetermined, but a shit ton. Maybe we will walk to meet each other one day up there, in a high mountain meadow full of paintbrush.

For me the *now* of *what sort of stories do we tell now* has had a long run-up. One *now* after which the writing could never be the same was the 2016 election. I am the child of a violent, alcoholic, physically and sexually abusive malignant narcissist (with a little borderline personality disorder thrown in) who resembles Trump in so many ways that after three years of this presidency I can scarcely remember my father. Climate chaos and my growing awareness of both the impending catastrophe and my role in it has been a rolling *now* over the last eight to ten years.

Also in that time, I have had the life-altering opportunity to teach in the Low Rez MFA program at the Institute of American Indian Arts in Santa Fe, in a community that is 75 percent Native American. There I have learned a thing or two about the history of my country (not that I was *so* naive before). I have learned how denial and the whitewashing of history is embedded so deep within us, so deep inside our very language, that it feels like a continuous excavation to get anywhere near the actual America where we reside, to understand the crimes it/we are committing every day. Yesterday, not only did the Feds give polluters license to pollute here in this moment when everybody is just for the love of god trying to *breathe*, but they also moved to disestablish the Mashpee Wampanoag reservation on Cape Cod in an old-fashioned land grab.

I'm not saying the virus isn't huge. Here are the numbers of the dead, a fraction of what will be the total. Here we are in our houses, for weeks, with no thought of leaving. But because of my experience with my father, I knew Trump would not be satisfied until he had caused massive, unimaginable damage (until he shot someone on 5th Avenue and got away with it). All the novels and memoirs I read from the IAIA students detail the brokenness of our systems so thoroughly I will never be able to unsee those schisms. The pandemic feels, to me, inevitable, the natural expression of greed and corruption gone completely unrestrained. Late-stage capitalism, *indeed*.

So my work, since Trump, since Kavanaugh, since Greta Thunberg's trip across the ocean, since my own trip to the fracking fields of North Dakota—on the one hand there is an urgency, and a kind of freedom within that urgency to speak out, to not be polite, an *if not now, when*? But there are also just a bunch of things that feel not all that worth writing about anymore. I know this gets tricky. I know most stories can be made to matter, or I used to know that. I said a long time ago, after

Cowboys Are My Weakness came out and I was accused of setting feminism back fifty years (for heaven's sake), that I believed feminism is meaningless if it is not every woman's right to her own story, whatever that story may be. On the other hand, what I say to myself every thirty seconds at IAIA is, "Shut the fuck up for a minute, white girl, this is not your time to talk."

To answer much more simply, it's hard to write, these weeks, about anything that is not in some way COVID-related. Since *Deep Creek* I've been working on a collection of short stories, and my character, Maggie, is a retired clinical psychologist who spent decades working with lifers in maximum security prisons and even one supermax. Now she trains young PsyDs who are about to go into prisons. These stories came out of an opportunity I had to work with eight lifers on storytelling at the California Men's Colony. I was thinking last night that Maggie has exactly the right attitude for a good COVID story. I feel lucky to not be so deep into a book, in other words, that it can't accommodate what is happening now.

I love your descriptions of putting students back in their bodies. I take, in a way, the opposite approach, where I refuse to let them (in first draft) say anything about themselves at all. I make them find themselves in an object, a stretch of river, or the bark of a tree, or the face of the woman at the checkout line at Walmart. Nouns, nouns, nouns, I tell them, I want nothing but the nouns you encounter, and when I get to experience the stuff of your world through your senses, I will come to know you as well.

Of all my work, teaching is the most important to me, but until COVID I always had to travel to do it (hello Zoom!) and I have tried to make some offsetting carbon cuts too. Not having children was the big one, but I keep my thermostat at sixty in the winter, and I don't have a clothes dryer. I bought a used Prius strictly for the non-snowy months to get me to Santa Fe or the Denver airport and back. I always add the carbon-offset tax to my plane tickets on the United site, gestures that feel pathetic when I line them up this way. And I love to go, I cannot lie. A new place makes me want to move my pen across the page like nothing else. Before COVID, I would have said if I stopped flying into the unknown my writing would suffer (to say nothing of my psyche). But after three weeks looking hard at the familiar, I am not as sure it's true. Months from now it might flip back the other way. But there is much to be learned from this semi-confinement. Of this I am sure.

None of us knows where this will end, or what will remain of the lives we've known when it's over. I feel like my job right now is to focus on the nouns. The guy at the gas station who told me Bill Gates invented the virus in a laboratory; my dog Henry, set free in the canyon, following his nose; today's walk up to the Ivy Creek Trailhead, two hours during which no plane passed overhead; this morning's avocado eggs with the very last of last summer's green chilies; my five-year-old hen, delivering me the first egg in six months, since the day she started growing her winter feathers, doing her best to help feed us during the pandemic. I think we may have lambs in a week or two, and that will be another adventure.

What about you? What are you writing? What are you feeling urged to write? I tried most of the afternoon to work on an essay and got mostly nowhere, but in correspondence the words come more easily. Perhaps we will all emerge from the pandemic, those of us who do, with books of letters...that could be beautiful, don't you think? How we were, together apart.

In friendship,
Pam

March 30, 2020

Hey there Pam,

How we were, together apart. This last line of yours had me weeping last night—equal parts grief and gratitude. Just days ago, the internet meant isolation and distraction, and now it's an agent of infinite intimacies. And these letters—they feel as necessary as air.

But if these letters were to be read later, as a chronicle of the times, I would be intensely aware that we are two healthy white women in respectful, loving relationships who have the enormous privilege of doing meaningful work from home, with plenty of food socked away and some of the most beautiful and accessible wildlands all around. Like you, I worry that our voices are the last voices that need to be heard right now.

But that's not quite right, is it? Our stories still matter. Who knows which stories will change the world? What if *Cowboys Are My Weakness* opens some white girl's eyes to possibilities beyond Tinder, Starbucks, the mani-pedi? What if it leads her to make and tend her own fire?

My life was changed by two stories written by privileged white people roaming the wilderness: Ed Abbey's *The Monkey Wrench Gang* and your *Cowboys Are My Weakness*. *The Monkey Wrench Gang* turned me into a wilderness activist. (Speaking of Abbey: where your first book was criticized for not being feminist enough, my book that responded to Abbey's other popular book, *Desert Solitaire*, was criticized for being *too* feminist—a real ball-biter, apparently.) But *Cowboys* was a book that convinced me it wasn't enough to follow men around in the wilderness, to heed their advice on how to stack the rope or field-dress an elk. Your stories inspired me to find my own way, trust my own instincts.

I, too, was the daughter of a narcissist and abuser. My father was an alcoholic and although he wasn't overtly physically violent, he was still sexually and physically reckless as hell with me. The last thing I wanted was to spend a day in the duck blind with him. And yet I wanted to follow him in the mountains, or on the river, though he never taught me to read a map or paddle the canoe. For all the hunting he did, he never taught me to handle a gun.

Then I read *Cowboys* and, oh, how I related. I had managed to make my own pack string of terrible backcountry love affairs—each one modeled after my relationship with my father. I took charge then, and learned everything I could about self-reliance in the wild. Soon I was climbing and hunting with other women. Eventually I made better choices about men, too—as partners both in romance and adventure. I grew more marbled into the land. It became less about me and more about the natural world. This led to Terry Tempest Williams' *Pieces of White Shell*, which led to learning more about the real Native Utahns who were displaced from lands I had been led to believe were mine by birth—as an American, and as a sixth-generation Mormon. Soon I was reading Simon Ortiz, Louise Erdrich, Joy Harjo.

It is through stories that I evolved as a human, an author, an activist. White people's stories were the first to save my ass—I was a terrible version of myself before books like yours and Abbey's. Reading them freed the land from my father's domain. I grew past his example and kept going, deeper into the wild.

Holding all of this, I wrote *Desert Cabal* as a response to *Desert Solitaire*. This was on the heels of Trump, Kavanaugh, Me Too. It was after five Native nations had come together with a vision for lasting protection of the Bears Ears. What an experience, to see so many white public lands advocates defer to the Bears Ears Inter-Tribal Coalition, to

29

Native voices. The movement forged my friendship with Regina Lopez-Whiteskunk, former Ute Mountain Ute councilwoman and former co-chair of the Bears Ears Coalition and all-around gem of a human being. She wrote such a beautiful epilogue for *Cabal*. She sometimes joined me on book tour, where we shared our cause and our stories about our relationship with wild places. Had my father been in the audience during one of our conversations, he wouldn't have understood a word.

What am I writing now? There's this second memoir about how a woman like me, with my need to be swallowed whole by the wilds, managed confinement at home with an epileptic child. The book has festered because I believed my predicament to be minor compared to everything else that's happening in the world. But in this new age of overt hatred for all things female, my sense of captivity as a mother also speaks, I think, to how unnatural we've made motherhood by confining it to the domestic.

So I started over, mid-pandemic. The new writing is close to the bone. It's a book my daughter can read and feel proud of. The old story would have left her feeling responsible for my sense of entrapment, and embarrassed for my being so unstable.

Here's my dirty little secret: I *live* for dystopian

narratives. Lately, I've turned to world-gone-to-hell works by women—often women of color. Louise Erdrich's *Future Home of the Living God*. Octavia Butler's *Parable of the Sower*. Alexis Wright's *The Swan Book*. Megan Hunter is white, but I have read *The End We Start From* three times. It's like *The Road*, except the mother isn't vilified by the author having her check out, as in Cormac McCarthy's nuclear holocaust. Instead, she breastfeeds her kid while rising seas flood much of England, with everyone stepping on one another to get to high ground. What I love about these books is what I love about what is happening in our letters, and in communities everywhere: the intimacies, the refusal to go fully feral. In this instance I equate ferality with independent survival at all costs. Which is so different than wildness, in which there is interdependence aimed at the survival of a whole pack or herd—indeed, an entire ecosystem.

Things are likely going to get worse. More people will sicken or die. More species will go extinct. Corporations and politicians will commit more human and environmental atrocities. The more scared and insecure people feel, the scarier and meaner they will become. Whatever dystopia unfolds around us, I refuse to be that kind of person. I told Ruby that, no matter what happens, let's seek out what's sweet—the hummingbird's nest, the asparagus bursting on the ditch. In response, Ruby logged on to a doomsday prepper site and made a list of all the freeze-dried treats with a crazy long shelf life. She printed the list, handed it over. The title: "Desserts for the Apocalypse."

This pandemic was indeed inevitable— although the number of lives lost or rendered barely worth living was *not*. Those who have been hit hardest are the same who will suffer the most from climate collapse, species extinctions, and the one percent who say "let them eat cake", even though Queen Marie, another woman vilified inside HIStory, never uttered those words.

This is no dystopian fiction, no single nation's revolution—although we are dangerously close to both. But what sweetness might we find here, in this unprecedented era? What basic nouns now taste like confections?

Soup. Home. Stories.
Spotted owl. Soap.
Egg. Sky. Ballot.

As ever,
Amy

March 31, 2020

Hi Amy,

A couple weeks ago, right before we began corresponding, you posted a few heart-stoppingly beautiful paragraphs about how grateful you were to be hunkered down with your husband and child. I reposted it because it was the truest thing I had seen since the beginning of the pandemic.

At that point I had been busy surviving. Stockpiling cartons of bone broth and raw cashews and counting the days (five, six, seven) since a stranger had hugged me or shaken my hand. It occurred to me, hours later, I ought to have asked permission to repost something so personal, so I did, and you wrote back "it's all personal now, isn't it?" I thought, right, so *that* is the name for this feeling of possibility in my chest.

Not that you need me to tell you this, but this is exactly the moment to write your motherhood memoir, from this place between the world as it was and the world as whatever it will be after. It's hard to imagine it otherwise.

If anyone had told us three months ago that, before summer came, the entire country and most of the world would give up bars and restaurants, massages, gyms, professional sports, airplanes, the Olympics, and movie theaters, we wouldn't have believed it. And though the consequences will be enormous, those of us fortunate enough to not be on the front lines of health care or food delivery have slipped into stay-at-home rather easily. Some of us are learning how much less we need. Some of us are learning different ways to define a life. I hear my own privilege in those sentences, but I don't know how to get around it. I am losing income by the truckload, like most people, but I am safe and warm in my sturdy house.

All of these letters are about remaking. Maybe fighting your way through your memoir will help you (continue to) remake motherhood into something that suits you and Ruby, coincident with the pandemic remaking our relationship to illness, immunity, and (we hope) health care as a human right. COVID is showing us what anyone with an abusing father or a sick kid already knows: that right now is all there has ever been, that the future is made of soap bubbles. The post-COVID world will be full of beauty and immense suffering, and in this way it will resemble the pre-COVID world, except more so. Maybe post-COVID we will be more conscious. Maybe being truly conscious will turn out to be the best feeling of all.

I'm moved, both by what you said about *Cowboys* and to find my name in the same sentence as Abbey's. *Desert Solitaire* was a touchstone for me before I ever laid eyes on the canyon country. I wrote Ed my first fan letter ever, and he sent me a postcard, with a drawing of the vulture. He thanked me for my letter, said "may great good fortune befall you." (Probably what he said to all the outdoorsy girls.) I tried to put my hands on that postcard just now, but that task may require my morning brain. I give his books credit for getting me out here, out to this landscape I was meant for, though he's only part of the story. Still, it would be hard for me to name a single writer that had more influence, not so much on my writing as on my life.

Yesterday a friend asked me to write a thing I didn't want to write by saying "everybody knows that's what you're good at." Maybe COVID gives us permission to stop spending all our time doing what we're good at. Maybe COVID is an opportunity to suck. Or to push the things we're good at so near to the cliff's edge we are in danger of them sucking. If everything is personal, then everything is dangerous and everything is possible beyond our wildest dreams.

When I worked in the prison, I could not get over the clarity I saw in my students' eyes. These were *the* eight men, the psychologist felt, out of hundreds, who had the best chance of going before the prison board and telling their stories of reform convincingly enough that they would be granted release. They had all accomplished the first part of their sentence—nineteen or twenty-five or thirty-five to life. They'd had some time to think about who they wanted to be in the world. This was California, so they had used their time to become Zen Buddhists, Reiki masters; one man got his PhD in philosophy. They had each murdered someone a long time ago. Now they were as clear-eyed and conscious as anyone I have ever met. Most of them had grown up in Watts, which is to say, the school-to-prison pipeline had been against them since they drew their first breath. They had paid for their crimes with the largest part of their lives, and now there was only honesty, in every word, in every gesture. They let me see all the way in, all the way down. They gave me and each other their complete attention at a level I didn't know existed. When I would leave the prison after a ten-hour day, I would see the Californians out watering their succulents or stopping by the Jamba Juice and it was unclear to me which world was the real one, or in which I belonged.

"Desserts for the Apocalypse" tells me Ruby is a girl after my own heart. I hope to meet her one day when we all come out of our caves again. This urge to love each other, to love everyone and everything, how much of it will we carry forward, when every second thought is not being able to breathe? A lot of it, I hope.

And now I am thinking of Eric Garner, which makes me think of the children in China (and LA for that matter) looking up and seeing blue sky. I was in Chengdu once, on my way to Tibet, and it was so polluted it was like *Blade Runner*, nighttime even in the day. What if everything *were* personal? What a world we could make if we held on to that.

More to come,
Pam

Hi Pam,

I'm back, after a computer disaster. How I missed our back-and-forth. Devin, Ruby, and I—along with most of the residents on our rugged and remote little mesa—just had our blood drawn to test for the virus. We'll be notified who has antibodies and who doesn't, then we'll all be tested again in two weeks. Until then, the whole county is under strict stay-at-home orders. Many have refused to be tested. Some folks believe it's a plot to steal our DNA and use it for some dark bio-warfare scheme, and many simply don't like to be told what to do. I confess, the whole thing inspired some paranoia—in town, we were bottlenecked into a controlled maze of orange cones, with all the other streets closed. There were many checkpoints manned by people in Tyvek suits and masks—I hardly recognized anyone. It was something right out of one of those dystopian novels. Maybe I won't love them so much anymore.

The free, countywide testing was offered by a pair of one-percenters who own a home in

Telluride and a biotech firm in Asia. They saw an opportunity here, to isolate and test in a way that no other US municipality has been able to. The whole effort was a feat of collaboration and coordination, but its coziness with deep pockets had *The Atlantic* and other news outlets writing disdainfully about how proximity to privilege made it possible. But there's also the hope that we'll learn how this virus behaves, how bodies respond to it over time. Also missed in most of those reports is that the west end of our county is way poor and way underserved—and they were given the opportunity to be tested, too. My paranoia melted when we arrived at the end of the maze to see our local doctors, medics, firefighters, elected officials, and so many other volunteers working together for the community—and the rest of us peering over our masks, waiting our turn under a wild windy sky. I felt waves of possibility then, about how much more we'll rely on one another, post-corona.

Pre-corona. Post-corona. It sounds so archaeological—like pre-Columbian, post-Clovis. The dinosaurs had their meteor, the Ancestral Puebloans had their drought. This virus, and how we respond, will be what defines us.

Since you last wrote, my computer exploded, literally. I lost all kinds of work, including one of your letters. Just weeks ago, this would have felt cataclysmic. Ditto for the loss of good French roast, a dental cleaning every six months, camping on a certain stretch of river. Now, the loss of these things is inconvenient and problematic but it's not the loss of air or water. Not the scarcity of food, or friendship. Not the erasure of environmental protections, of health and human services. Which are what should have mattered most all along.

What helped ease my frustration was you spurring me on to write this next book. I thought the story was the severe, undiagnosed postpartum depression, the terrible marriage, the sick baby that had me cooped up inside. I couldn't bear to tell it. So that's why I dove into doomsday narratives! I could say to myself, "Oh, look at that man getting his face eaten by zombies. My life could be so much worse."

But the story is not about how I survived. It's about how I thrived. It started when my neighbors put me on a horse because they needed help moving some cows. Soon I was helping them move stock regularly. I was ridiculous at first; I had no idea what I was doing and there were heavy doses of Benadryl and a steroid inhaler involved. I was deathly allergic to horses, you see. Summers and weekends spent on my grandparents' ranch in Idaho were spent mostly indoors when there was nothing I wanted more than to be neck-deep in the animals. Especially the horses. The one time I sneaked out and went for a gallop on my grandfather's buckskin landed me in the hospital for a week.

One day I forgot to take the drugs before getting on the horse and *voilà*, my animal allergies had vanished. I still had a child who was often in crisis, but I learned to escape at times. The rebound didn't feel hard-earned enough to write about— which was me buying into patriarchy's belief that my experience is irrelevant. So I tried to hang it on something bigger: the ancient women warriors of the Siberian steppes. They were some of the earliest horse people, and fearsome. Their mummies are—thanks to climate chaos—being spit out of the melting permafrost. This, as COVID creeps across the planet.

I need to carry the story. Sure, those women can ride around in the background and wave their swords and shields, but if it's all personal, post-corona, then we must claim our stories in a way we couldn't before. And maybe this is part of what you mean about now giving ourselves permission to do things we suck at, like riding a horse or mothering. We can still take it right to the cliff's edge, into the danger zone, where the impossible alchemizes into possible. Our wildest dreams, indeed.

You mention consciousness and clarity. That is exactly what being on a horse, in rough country, taught me. There was danger all right: I just wrote the book's opening scene, about the day the Arabian and I came upon a mountain lion who wouldn't back down. We were out in front of the herd, setting the pace as we headed up the mountain, and that cat walked out in front of us. The horse and I became one in that moment—we had a job to do, and that was to get two hundred head of Black Angus cows and calves to the grazing allotment before the sun got too high in the sky. So we played chicken and marched right up on the lion. We won, when the lion backed off into the brush. In those blood-dancing moments certain narratives from outside myself wanted to prevail— like "mountain lions are a horse's greatest fear" and "oh god, I am no cowboy and this horse is gonna throw me and run." Now both those statements are fairly accurate, but at the time I wondered, what if there's another story, between this horse, this lion, and me? What if I actually know what to do because those ancient women warrior genes are singing in my cells? What then?

So often these days, what I care about, what I want to write about, is eclipsed by breath. Can my lungs get enough air if I am infected with COVID-19? Will that air be breathable, given the pollution from cars and factories, given the smoke from the now vast and frequent wildfires? I bawl when I see images of people standing at hospital and nursing home windows—singing, praying, waving to the person inside, sometimes saying goodbye. That illicit ride on my grandfather's buckskin put me in an oxygen tent, where I was pumped full of steroids and antibiotics, all to keep my six-year-old lungs open. I remember too well how distraught I was by the distance between my grandfather and me, as he stood outside my window of the tiny hospital in tiny Malad, Idaho, as he held my little sister (who wasn't allowed in the hospital) and they both waved to me through the glass. The nurses hovered and fussed—trying to calm me down so my O$_2$ levels would rise.

I was in this same situation when I returned from Mongolia last fall. I came down with a deadly pneumonia that required three rounds of antibiotics to defeat. For weeks I was bedridden. And six months later, I still don't feel quite right. But the air there—in Ulaanbaatar, Mongolia's capital—my god, was it foul. There are four hulking smokestacks in the center, disgorging black, oily smoke to generate coal-fired power, and you feel lathered in it, inside and out. Everyone in the city coughs, hacks, spits up chunks. Children are dying left and right from pneumonia attributed to the air quality.

If it were up to the Mongolian people, they'd all be nomadic herdsmen and they'd be out in the wilderness, burning yak dung in their little stoves, but their superpower neighbors have put dirty fuels before human and animal health.

The Mongolians believe in three worlds: one is (ironically) the Eternal Blue Sky, ruled by birds of prey. There is the Earthly World, where herds and packs of terrestrial animals roam. And the Underworld, where fantastic beasts lurk—the animals painted in the backs of caves, the animals in our dreams. But here in America, we've lost our connection to the Underworld. Few people make the trip anymore.

Ruby shakes as the Earth shrugs. There's no airflow with each seizure. And yet she holds the whole of this strange new world with all the acreage in her heart. It helps, I believe, that she dreams of a white mother wolf that nuzzles her throat, of foxes leading her into a primordial forest. I tremble, just describing this to you. I know you know what I mean. The animals, whatever realm, keep it real. They keep it personal. They sometimes save our lives.

The extinctions, the migrations. The school shootings, the wildfires. Ruby's grief and anger are different from mine because she's the one hiding under her desk when the school goes on lockdown

during a drill. The one who looks ahead and wonders if her house will burn in a wildfire, if college
will even be a thing.

But Ruby and other young women—they
give me seismic hope. They are not Pollyannas,
nor is that the kind of optimism they inspire. We
lament the time younger generations spend staring at techno-screens, but it's made the world less
of an abstraction for them. They know in a cyber-
visceral way how the world is ailing, how our
leaders are failing. And that's why they scare the
shit out of Trump, McConnell, the Koch brothers,
the Harvey Weinsteins and Kavanaughs. They are
clear-eyed; they see that the emperor never wore
a single thread. With our help, the young women
are our best weapon. The old sad sacks of flesh
who would mine more coal and kill more kids so
they can eat caviar or pangolin another day, they
don't stand a chance against the girls who sail
across oceans, who are guarded by white wolves.

The state of Colorado required Ruby's dad and
me to watch a "healthy co-parenting" video as part
of our divorce process. The video shows changes in
the brain that occur when our anger/fear/anxiety
gets triggered. At that moment, the reptilian brain
takes over—we are in fight-or-flight and from
that place we cannot resolve conflict, cannot feel
compassion, cannot create solutions. The video

points to studies that show how taking seven deep breaths kicks you back into the frontal cortex, into the arena of reasoning, calm, and empathy.

This part of the brain is where the clear-eyed girls and fantastic beasts live—I'm sure of it.

Maybe that's how we live now. Seven breaths at a time.

Back at you,
   Amy

Good morning Pam,

I know it's your turn to write, but my OCD, middle-of-the-night thought was this: even with all the context I've shared, it still sounds self-absorbed to claim that motherhood was confining, devastating. I am, after all, an educated white woman in America. I get to work at home in a loft dedicated to writing, and when I need a break I can walk out onto a little balcony and see wildness for hundreds of miles. Standing there, a pair of golden eagles will buzz my scalp and send my heart soaring. Such gifts. At least for now.

What I know for sure is that privilege doesn't spare you from trauma, although it can lessen the blow, and the aftermath. If the definition of apocalypse is "an event that causes damage or destruction on a catastrophic scale," then becoming a mother was just that. Everything I knew about myself was totaled, and whatever trauma I still had from childhood, from past relationships, well, this eclipsed them all. I have no idea how I wrote the second half of my memoir *Trespass* from inside of that, but after it was finished, Ruby got increasingly ill and this derailed her "developmental milestones" (whatever the hell those were—the docs would use the term and look at me as though I had done something wrong).

I put down the pen, picked up a sponge, and started cleaning uber-homes in Telluride. I was dead inside.

One day, I am scrubbing away when our mutual friend Craig Childs calls and asks what I am doing. I say I have my head in an oven coated with Easy-Off and I'm choking on the fumes. He says, "WTF, girl?" I hang up on him (we have that kind of sibling thing). He calls back. He tells me that the MFA program he teaches in is seeking a nonfiction fellow—an already established writer to teach in exchange for an advanced degree. "This is your ticket out," he said. "You'll be able to teach instead of clean."

I almost hung up again. I couldn't imagine being able to complete the application, let alone be granted the position.

Craig was relentless. Finally, I applied, and I received the fellowship—perhaps the single greatest gift of my life because it required that I write again. It was not easy to find the time and space to think about stories when Ruby was so unwell and collectors hounded me for unpaid medical bills. But I kept at it. I worked on the motherhood memoir as my thesis. Ruby got worse and the writing never fully came together, but at least I was in the habit again. And I was teaching—which I love. It was enough to pull my head out of the oven.

Craig. He not only saved my life, he introduced me to Devin, one of his oldest and dearest friends. Devin is the man who stands apart from all the others I've tangled with. He is kind and creative and true and not an hour goes by in which I am not head-over-heels thankful for and admiring of him. Craig also introduced me to you, and while we have only just met (in letters!), this conversation has been the only way I can bear to look back at what is no longer. The only way I can look ahead, and wonder what to take with us when we can leave the house again. It feels like stuffing a backpack for a multi-day hike, or cramming gear into a dry bag for a week on the river. My priorities are pared down, coming into focus fast.

Who knows what else has to go. Not the pen and paper—that's for sure. And I'll always, no matter what, make room for these relationships, these conversations.

They are, to circle back again, as necessary as air.

Abrazos,
            Amy

PS It's my father's birthday. He's been dead twenty years now. He was a conservative, except when it came to his own appetites. I suspect he would have loved Trump but even if he'd hated him, there's no way he'd have voted for Hillary.

Dear Amy,

Oh my lord so many things to respond to. I have missed you too. Craig, dear Craig. We were at an awards dinner, maybe it was in Montana, right after his first child was born. I asked him how he was, and he looked at me with his bright and kind feral eyes, and said, "Not only have I lost my best friend, but now I am forced to live inside the bright beam of my wife's ferocious motherhood." Craig and I have had many conversations over the years, but it was this one that made me understand he was one of us, one of me.

I am so *FOR* the motherhood story, in all its catastrophe and love. We lie about so many things in this country. Our history, our values, our fears. We also lie about motherhood. We lie about it as much as we lie about our embedded racism. It is a dirty lie that a woman is selfish if she doesn't want to have a child, or that she is not a whole person, or whatever other shit they say. There is at least an equally compelling argument that by not having children she is being unselfish. I know women for whom motherhood is the greatest experience of their lives, and I know at least an equal number of women for whom it is a disaster. It was a disaster for my mother and she told me so every day. "I gave up everything I loved for you." It was a hard thing to hear, but I know I am better off, I am a better, clearer, more honest person, because she did not pretend it was a fucking picnic, she did not walk around with that glazed look in her eyes so many women have, saying how awesome motherhood is when anyone can see they are dying inside.

What I want most for the world after COVID is for all of us to stop lying. I want that for myself. You are a truth teller and your particular combination of ferocity and compassion will make the book work, even though it will feel like you are walking really close to the edge. What great book was ever written without walking really close to the edge? None of them.

Motherhood *is* apocalyptic, or at least it can be. It was for my mother, and it would have absolutely been for me. My mother's mother died in childbirth, and so it was understandable my mother believed she died when I was born. Would I have felt the same sense of life being over? I didn't know, but I wasn't going to find out.

I got free of my father's house, against incredible odds—I don't believe that's an exaggeration.

I made it out with my crooked femur, and scar tissue covering my cervix, and some shred of myself still intact. In the decades when I could have had a child, and by that I mean biologically, I would not, could not, have given up my freedom for anything. I had a friend who said to me, "But Pam, when you look into your baby's eyes, it will be your Tibet." I have no doubt looking into one's own baby's eyes can be any number of powerful things, but one thing it is not is Tibet.

Everything *is* personal and the personal *is* political. I am consistently amazed that all these years after *Roe v. Wade*, as the planet begins to really die in earnest, women are *still* shamed for not having children, shamed even more for not wanting them.

I know this isn't the point of your book. I'm not confusing what you are saying with my own personal agenda (perhaps a little). I'm saying your story matters on every level: personal, political, environmental. It's great the Mongolian women are in there, adding a layer, informing your decisions, functioning as metaphors. It's also great you know they are not the story and you are.

Motherhood is the thing that took you all the way down, and then you rose up into love. That's the only story for any of us who have gone all the way to the bottom, including my friends at the

California Men's Colony. *What if there is another story between me and this cliff and this mountain lion*, indeed. This is what survivors do. They find that other story. What if we all have those ancient Mongolian warrior women cells singing in our veins, and this pandemic, this apocalypse of a presidency, are the clarion calls to use them.

Every time you write even the smallest thing about Ruby, your love for her swirls up from the sentences like smoke from a campfire. She is your favorite animal. She is your connection, or one of them, to the animals of the underworld and to the animals of all the worlds. She came from your animal body, and it almost killed you. But it didn't, and you rose up into hard-won love.

If this were another time and place, Ruby would be the one telling us how to live and we would listen. And that IS why we have a chance. Because of Greta, and Ruby, Emma González, Jamie Margolin, Isra Hirsi. They have already gone all the way down and come all the way back into love. We need to stand with them in whatever way possible. By virtue of the leather on our faces, we need to have their backs.

My animals have taught me so very many things. How to live, how to love, how to die, and maybe most importantly, how to be with the dying. They have taught me how to administer care. They have taught me how to wag. They have taught me what to be afraid of, and much more importantly, what is not so scary after all. They have shown me I am a creature. Going forward, I want to be more creaturely. I want to sleep like a creature. And walk on the Earth like one. I want to get better at caring for myself and others in a creaturely fashion.

I'm glad you got/get to ride those horses. I have only one horse now who is too elderly to ride (but not to love on every day) and a miniature donkey who wants to make trouble with everybody. A young horse has been on my mind for a couple of years now, before this lockdown. An Icelandic, I am thinking. When I think of them, a phrase you used about Ruby comes to mind. *All the acreage in her heart.*

One of the great joys in my life, this last decade or two, has been becoming second/replacement/surrogate mother/mentor to a whole mess of young women and a few young men. It begins in the grad programs, of course, but then turns into something more. There is a picture of me dancing with about six of them at my wedding. Maybe I will attach it. It turns out, when it comes to mothering, twenty-three to thirty is my sweet spot. I can help a twenty-eight-year-old artistic outdoorsy woman believe in her own power like nobody's business, and the reward turns out to be mine. We have the kind of whole-self fun together I wouldn't allow myself when I was their age, though I was running rivers and skiing chutes and doing all manner of ostensibly "fun" things, trying to keep up with the boys. Rather than making me wish I had had children, these young writers make me glad I saved up all my mothering for them. I know enough to do it well now, which is to say, I know enough to know when to speak and when to be quiet.

And a purely practical aside: Are you taking an osha tincture? I have badly scarred lungs from my many trips to super altitudinous Asia. I've taken it every day for a month and I feel really well.

Also, I nearly cut my little finger off yesterday morning, trying to catch a knife I was in the process of dropping. I cried because I was afraid I would have to go to the hospital, I cried because it was such a dumb move, and let's face it, I cried because it was a good opportunity. But then I found some butterfly closures and so far, at least, so good. In my river guiding days, of course, I would have sewn it up using baling twine and my teeth.

I'm going to send this now, though I could go on and on, there is more in your letters I didn't get to, but I want to do some thinking about the underworld. I'm also going to send Craig a note of gratitude, though he is probably at the bottom of a canyon somewhere.

I await your response, as one of my first boyfriends used to say, with bait on my breath. (God, there it is again!)

In the name of clean air for all of us,

Pam

April 5, 2020

Helloooo Paaam…

I'm writing from inside the wind tunnel while being sandblasted by desert pollens. I want to take a fork to my itchy, swollen eyes.

Well. Your grandmother died in childbirth. My grandmother, my mother's mother, died on the night of Ruby's birth. And your mother sounds a lot like my mother, who, in my early twenties—when I told her my father had molested me—said that being a mother had just about ruined her life. At the time I was devastated by her comment but now I see the truth of it: when she had children, her needs and desires no longer mattered—especially to my father. It wasn't me she was rejecting, but the bleak conditions of motherhood, as prescribed by a culture that doesn't value women as much as it worships men.

I admire that you knew enough about yourself not to have a kid. I have cherished my freedom, but I didn't learn how to honor it until I'd given it all away. I was so busy proving to Ruby's father that I would be a kick-ass mother that I never stopped to think about whether or not I could be a good one, if the conditions of my life and marriage were such that I could thrive—so that in turn, my child could thrive. I'm plagued by this worry that I've shortchanged Ruby, that I may have even caused her health issues by failing all tests of maternal aptitude.

For one thing, I leave her, a lot. And every time I'm booked to go somewhere I'm dying to explore—that I must write about—my daughter goes into crisis. Which leads to another dirty little secret: I've never canceled. I go anyway. When she was diagnosed with Graves' disease at six years of age, I ran off to the French caves, to commune with the animals painted there. When she was diagnosed with epilepsy, I went to the Isle of Arran, off of Scotland. And when her epilepsy worsened, I headed for Mongolia, and jumped on a horse. I can't really explain it, and maybe I wouldn't go if her dad weren't such a good caregiver, but I know that my staying gets all-consuming and that's not good for either Ruby or me. There is a price to pay for my going—from other mothers, especially. My closest friends and Devin know better. They're like just GO already, or you'll crumble. We'll help cover for you, but you gotta go. And Ruby, bless her. Much as she hates it, she knows that if I don't go, I'll wither.

You said, despite your mother, you turned out all right. More than all right, I'd say. And I think Ruby, despite my maternal shortcomings and because of what she's been through, is one helluva human. You nailed it when you observed she's my favorite animal. She is that, for sure, which is saying a lot, because I love animals infinitely. Love all the ways they burrow or charge into my life.

What haunts me most in this discussion is that your friend compared your would-be child to Tibet. Oh my god. The more we refuse to read from patriarchy's motherhood script, the more pushback there is. Last Thanksgiving, two guys who worked on wilderness issues with me—good guys, and like-minded, I thought—joined us for dinner. One asked what I was writing. I mentioned the second memoir, my obsession with the ancient women warriors. They asked questions but it was more like a cross-examination aimed at proving the project worthless—as in well, that's cute, but how could a story about mothers and the women warriors matter when we are trying to save the planet? I was sitting there, after two days of cooking, having yet to taste a bite of food because the attack was so steady. I finally stopped and said, "What the fuck are you guys doing? It's Thanksgiving, for godsake." How fitting, to have these guys declare eminent domain over this colonialist ritual in which we were all, I could suddenly see, inexplicably still participating. They of course sat back in their chairs and sighed. One even rolled his eyes. Their faces read, plain as day: "Here we go again. Another sad example of Me Too getting taken too far."

Now I am used to this kind of dismissal from men. But it is maddening to see it in the guys who are supposed to be on my side, who should value social justice every bit as much as eco-justice—because the two are inextricable unless you are saving wilderness purely for selfish reasons, as your own personal and privileged sanctuary. This is why *Desert Cabal* was so important for me to write. (One of these guys also made sure to tell me, at length, how disappointed he was in that book.) Because just as there is still considerable racism in the environmental movement, there's a boatload of sexism, too. Oh, did I get hate mail for *Cabal*. From men who believed I had no right to take on Abbey. And yet it was fine for Abbey to take on anything he damn well pleased. That double standard is alive and well still. And really, if you don't take women that seriously, if you don't examine how you diminish them in the workplace, at the dinner table, well then we're really not fighting for the same version of the world, are we?

Which leads me to something I didn't quite come clean about, earlier in this exchange. When I first read *Cowboys*, I threw it across the room. Now, I can be reactive and over-the-top about things, but I usually manage to circle back and say, "What was *that* about, Amy?" And I welcome the animals that come through dreams to show us a part of ourselves—for better or for worse. Of course, I love it when I get the elk medicine, or the big red stallion who breaks down my door. There is also the vulnerable little cottontail, and the sensual rattlesnake, full of the venom we need to kill our apathy, our disembodiment. But there are also black widows—which, when Ruby was young, infested my dreams (and our house too, I kid you not). That's another kind of poison, a kind of toxic dark feminine that sinks its fangs so fast I don't see it coming.

So I picked the book back up, went to therapy, talked about *Cowboys*. And then I could see the spider in me. Only then could I disentangle from a web of toxic relationships, from believing if only I were a better hunter-hiker-lover-cowgirl-climber-drinker then even the most absent man would suddenly, magically, become present. This eventually made me into another species altogether, embedded me in another kind of relationship altogether. So many books that I love—the most important ones in my life—I've had that reaction to. They open a door in me, offer the invitation to step through. I finally go, but not without a few animals as company, me kicking and screaming bloody murder.

Our stories are deeply personal. And, as you said, they are also political, environmental. Meaning the story of women is the story of the world. So, yes, let's draw our swords, nock our arrows. Let's ride. There are a few men who will go with us—and won't even tell us how to tack our horses. I'll diverge here to say that one thing I love about the ancient Scythian horsewomen is that, even though the Greeks both mythologized and vilified (two sides of the same coin, really) them as man-eating, baby-killing Amazons, their culture very much involved men—and the two genders were quite fluid, in terms of warring, hunting, training horses, raising children. In one tomb there might be a woman warrior buried with all kinds of armament, and in the next tomb a man laid to rest with none, cradling a child instead. In other tombs, there are men and women together—both with weapons, and sometimes children. But they always, always had horses, falcons, dogs. This is the life I believe will save us: the one where we are badass, and outside, moving across good ground. Where we can be moms and warriors and writers and lovers all at once.

Not to be too romantic here. Doing battle guarantees wounding. Wounding leaves scars. You have scar tissue on your cervix and I had so much scar tissue strangling my ovaries and uterus that all of those parts had to be cut out. There are still webs of the stuff in there, wrapped around my intestines, gluing my stomach muscles to my ribs and my ribs to my spine. It cannot be removed, because it grows right back and then some. All I can do is keep rolling around on various torture devices—balls, rollers, and hard pokey things like air hockey paddles—to keep my body moveable. These scars of ours are battle scars because they have everything to do with sex and violence.

And then there's the scar tissue in our lungs, from pneumonias, from high altitudes. (I, too, am taking osha tincture right now.) I hate feeling extra vulnerable to this virus, to know that the breath of another human could kill me. I mean, how dark is that metaphor? Breath *gives* life. Sustains it. Just weeks ago, it was a given joy to put our heads together—to share secrets, hushed jokes, a kiss. To see a friend and brush cheeks when you hug.

Oh, and there's the scar you'll no doubt have from the kitchen knife. I do hope that it heals up without a trip to the clinic or hospital. I'll be thinking about that, until you're healed.

We've survived sexual scarring, but our lung scars may do us in, if we're unfortunate enough to inhale the virus. The battle is twofold now, isn't it? We're fighting not only for room to breathe in our compressed lives but for the right to just *breathe*. What color your skin is and whether or not your governor kisses POTUS's ass determine whether you'll get a mask, a ventilator. Which in turn can decide if you live or die.

In my early twenties, after passing my EMT certification, I was bouldering in Little Cottonwood Canyon, outside of Salt Lake. I was in a grove of trees, below the climbing cliffs, when I heard a body hit the ground (an unmistakable sound), followed by the screams and wails of several men. I scrambled up a gulley and onto the next level of granite, where the routes were. A kid in his late teens had fallen from the top of a climb, onto the hard slab of stone at the base. There were three or four other climbing parties, all men, all older than me. And they were traumatized by what they'd seen—you might say hysterical, and rightly so. A few were frozen in place. One guy cradled the kid who fell and was trying to pour Gatorade in his mouth even though it was clear that the young man wouldn't make it. His brain was exposed, crushed. His neck was off to the side, and his belly ballooned with blood. Because there was a head injury, the body thrashed around, as if combative, but it was all reflex. The guy's climbing partner, another young man, was still holding the rope and figure eight, staring up at the route (weirdly, a route my uncle did the first ascent of, back in the sixties), mouth open. I show up and they all look at me with the most desperate faces. I thought, "But I'm just a small woman in Lycra." Then I remembered. I had trained for this.

I issued a few orders: Hey man, put down the Gatorade and tie the kid in, before he thrashes off this ledge we're on. You there, go call for help. And the rest of you, rig lines to get search and rescue up here because I saw them training last weekend and they were all huge and out of shape. There'll be more bodies piling up if we aren't prepared to haul them up ourselves.

Then I turned and kneeled next to the boy who was dying. Bodily fluids everywhere. By now his climbing partner was next to me, telling me that the kid had just gotten home from his mission the day before, that they'd celebrated his engagement to his girlfriend last night, and now this. Then the kid said, "So you can save him, right?"

By now the body was still. And the kid had been out of the country. He may have had unpro-tected sex, as many young people tend to, even on their Mormon missions. I could possibly become infected if I ingested his spit or puke or blood. I finally said I'd do chest compressions if someone else would do mouth-to-mouth. Everyone looked at me in shock, confusion, but no one volunteered.

I froze. I could not put my mouth on his. Now, the newer guidelines say that mouth-to-mouth isn't necessary—but back then, as you know, it was deemed essential to saving someone. So I'm standing there feeling like this kid's death was on my shoulders and everyone starts freaking out again but then one guy, a Rambo-type, steps forward and says he'll do it. For at least an hour, in the ninety-degree heat, he mouthed and I pumped. I vaguely remember the SAR mobile command unit pulling into the parking lot in the canyon below, and a balloon of a man waddling out with a megaphone, and barking something like, "Professionals have arrived. Please step away from the victim and we'll take it from here." And then came all kinds of big sweaty guys, juggling jump kits, stretchers, ropes.

It was the most singular, sacred thing, massaging that young man's heart and pumping oxygen to his very damaged brain. I knew he wouldn't recover, and of course he did not. What kept me working on him was that hope, that miracle, that we must always reach for when the stakes are high, because if we don't make every effort to help each other, then we've gone feral, which is not the same as wild—not here, anyway. Then we're living in the bleak, on Cormac McCarthy's *Road*. And as bad as things seem, giving in to that story will doom us all.

There are nights when my daughter's seizures keep going, when she gets blue in the face and I'm counting carefully how long the seizure lasts, because all that time she's not getting oxygen. And every time, I am tempted to think, "I'm just a small woman in flannel pajamas," because it doesn't feel right to be what so many people want me to be— which is the fierce mama bear. I love bears, and I've had a standoff with a sow grizzly with two cubs when we surprised one another on a trail in British Columbia, and she was the scariest, most awesome thing I've ever seen up close. But I'm not that bear. I am not an apex predator; I'm scrawnier, scrappier. I lack maternal instincts—which she clearly had a shit ton of. And I do wear flannel pajamas.

I'm sick of being pegged as the fierce mama bear because I fight fiercely for my kid. I am sick of being likened to the black widow, the original femme fatale, because I have had more than my fair share of failed relationships. So this is where the women warriors come in. They do sing in our veins, even now—I know, because I've heard them on those long nights, when I'm doing battle with epilepsy. I can feel that ghostly warhorse under my ass, that quiver full of arrows strapped to my thigh. I feel it alive in me—women who were almost animal, who embodied many animals, but never only one or the other. Right now I am a Steller's jay. Raucous, scolding. Like this mohawked bird, I rarely leave the forest canopy, which is my desk in the loft. Rarely do I descend to ground, and then only for food. But an hour from now I'll be another creature altogether.

Oh, and that photo you sent, with your students, at your wedding. It touches me so deeply. The kind of nurturing you're gifting to these young writers, the way you help them birth their stories into the world. This work we do, it's both fierce and tender. It is the work of the warrior/mother/animal who is wide awake, battling for a better world and whether those two guys at Thanksgiving know it or not, they won't save the planet without us.

So let's sharpen the blades. Let's be beautiful and maternal and brutal all at once.

For all things wild and wondrous,
Amy

April 9, 2020

Hi Amy,

I had a really shitty day Sunday. The cut on my hand opened up badly, because it did so great for the first twenty-four hours I decided I didn't have to pay attention to it anymore, and then right before bed, my friend Sarah wrote and told me the US had stopped giving out passports, ostensibly because of COVID, but when one follows the train we've been riding these last three years it is hard not to think of fascism and a military dictatorship where passport renewal might just cease to be a thing.

I know my passport doesn't expire until 2026, and that's enough time to know whether I can stay in this country and speak freely, or if I'll have to make a run for the border, so I thought it would be good to put my hand on my passport just to reassure myself it was there. But it WASN'T there, in the very back corner of my underwear drawer (clever, I know) where it usually resides. So I tore the bedroom apart. Every drawer upside down on the floor.

I thought, well, you've been running so hard this last year, it's probably in a backpack or suitcase or tote bag somewhere, so all of those were emptied and gone through, fast and frantically the first time, then more slowly and depressingly as the moon went across the sky. I tore apart my car, I tore apart all of my tax return paraphernalia. The underwear drawer again, and the sock drawer, and the T-shirt drawer in case I had decided to outsmart some imagined robber. And then my desk, and then the other desk, which is basically nobody's, and then my camera case. You get the idea.

It was about three a.m. when I started to cry, because I have known since spring of 2016 that this soulless ghoul of a man who doesn't admire anyone except dictators and himself, who millions of Americans chose to run this country; I have known he was going to get me. He is not even Trump to me, but my dead father come back to get me after all. I only thought I got away. I had these glorious forty years between leaving my father's house, and coming back to his house, only this time, weirdly, there are 330 million people and we are all in his house together. He has been waiting for me, I sobbed into my big dog's back, to make the one fatal mistake that would allow him to get me. There I was, arranging all the cans of

Hatch chilies in the cabinet according to their expiry date, figuring out how to get fish delivered along with a case of Meyer lemons for their vitamin C. There I was, with my thirty-year-old river trip first-aid kit butterfly closures and enough of the only dog food that doesn't give Henry the shits to last until August, my osha tincture and my bottle of thieves, my deep breathing exercises to stave off pneumonia. All that, and I lost my goddamn passport weeks (months?) before the US stopped giving them out forever, turning me into a sitting duck.

I did not wake Mike in the middle of the night to tell him this, though he would not have been angry if I had. I cried with the dog, and then I played Wordscapes on my phone until the sky got light.

Mike asked if the passport could be at the Davis apartment, and though it seemed impossible I could have been so careless as to leave it there in October when I got back from teaching in Mexico, I couldn't say for sure. Mike said Trump was so interested in getting the country reopened, even if the ultimate plan *is* to become like Russia, there would be at least a window where I could get a new passport. He reminded me that the US/Canadian border is the most porous in the world. *So many trees*, he said, without laughing, without saying I was crazy, without for one second or in even the smallest way implying I might be way too damaged to love.

When it got late enough in California to call a friend, I did, and he went over to my apartment, and sure enough there was my passport, in THAT underwear drawer, all the way in the back corner.

To be clear, I cried all night because other than the moment the knife entered my hand, I had not cried since the pandemic began. I had not cried about John Prine. About Terrence McNally. About the twelve thousand dead (and counting), about how much of this could have been avoided without those goddamn seventy days of lies and withholding and congressmen selling stocks, about how much harder it is going to be to make a living now. It had been weeks since I had cried about all the things I was crying about periodically before, like the babies in cages at the border, like the end of the Clean Air Act. *THE CLEAN AIR ACT*. About all of the things we have already talked about so I don't need to name them again.

But maybe the more important thing to say is that I *was* crying very specifically (and relentlessly) because I didn't know where my passport was, because I had misplaced the document that allowed me to GO. To run. To spend a month in Patagonia or a decade in Iceland. To buy a garlic farm in Kaslo, British Columbia, or a crumbling farmhouse on a Greek island. To fly to France, where I am supposed to be teaching a class in June (doubtful it will happen), to go anywhere other than this fracturing country which has become all too much like my father's house.

Which brings me back to motherhood, and an unplanned pregnancy, thirty years ago, in a good but not necessarily long-term relationship. But to make my decision about the viability of the relationship is to tell a lie. His name was Mike, too, and he was a good man, and went on to have a bunch of kids and horses and a good life with a woman much different from me. I terminated that pregnancy because the idea that I might not be able to run, to go to Mongolia, or Pittsburgh, or the grocery store knocked the wind out of me. It bent me in half. How much of it is the matrilineal curse of death by childbirth? How much of it is knowing that if I didn't keep running from my father's house it would be the end of me? And how much is for the pure joy that GOING affords me? This is a pie chart I don't know how to fill in.

I'm glad you get to go, glad the people closest to you understand. As for the mothers who look down their nose at you, fuck them. You are modeling for Ruby a woman who knows what she needs and who sometimes puts her needs before the needs society thinks she should prioritize. And let's face it, even with your going, you are there for Ruby, more and more fully than anyone else. And you get to be there as the fully embodied woman/writer/traveler/adventurer/mother you are, not some shell of yourself who is doing what everyone else thinks you should. It takes a village and it should take one. I turned out okay because I learned early there were many people in the world who had things to show me, to give me, to teach me. I learned in that process to say yes to the world.

And speaking of people we are telling to fuck off, if anyone said (or even implied) to my face that the Me Too thing has gone too far, I would go full Tasmanian devil on them, whether I had just cooked them a Thanksgiving meal or not.

Have you seen that CNN video of all the people going to church? If you have not, google *CNN, washed in the blood of Christ*. Watch the first woman interviewed and tell me if it isn't horror film scary, except more so. I mean, what is the difference between that clip and a horror film. Except we live in it now. It's real.

The story about the dead boy in Little Cottonwood is a stunner. And for all my river trips gone wrong and the decade in my life where I seemed to attract natural disasters (hurricanes, earthquakes, mudslides) I have never been close to anyone with a crushed skull, though I did sew a pirate's arm up once, from shoulder to elbow, using an awl, a thin leather string, and his tattoos to make sure I was keeping the lines straight.

There is nothing shameful about choosing your life. Whether it is choosing not to give mouth-to-mouth to an already dead kid, or going to Mongolia because that's what you need. We have big battles before us now and we have no time for so many of the things that held us back. One of those things for me is my incessant need to increase the degree of difficulty of any task exponentially to prove my worthiness. Things are tough enough, thank you, without your disparaging mothers or wilderness bros, or the ghost of my father or anyone else who will feel better about their selfish choices because of my silence.

Beautiful and brutal, introspective and ferocious. I am pretty sure the only way through is up high on the cantle, mane and tail flying. Trying to stay safe, trying to be invisible, can only lead to despair. The only time I feel really okay anymore is when I am fighting for the things I love, whether it's a student's manuscript, or protection for wolves and grizzly bears. Battling for a better world is the only occupation now and it is women's turn to lead the charge, maybe with a few good men in tow.

I hope all is well on your side of the San Juans and the wind has calmed a bit. It has here. Today was stupidly gorgeous, and we found a new hiking trail.

Be well, my friend.
Pam

Wowza Pam,

What a harrowing night you had. I am so sorry. Thank god for Wordscapes and dogs and the kindest words from a good man.

As you well know, it won't be the last.

Every day, there is another step taken without our permission, leading us deeper into a dictatorship that so many checks and balances were supposed to protect us from. Funny that we thought we'd dodge the tragic end that comes to every bloated empire.

Hence the woman who believes she's immune to the virus because she's covered with Christ's blood. That scene in *Carrie*, when Sissy Spacek comes out on the stage during the prom after she's gone on a killing spree and she's holding the knife? That's what sprung to mind. Her white dress, her pale skin, and her strawberry hair, all smeared with blood. Her face both deranged and virtuous.

But that is Hollywood. This is supposed to be reality. (I can't believe I just wrote that sentence in all seriousness.) Just think of that woman as she waltzes into church, then parades through Walmart, then Hobby Lobby. When the reporter asks her if she ever wonders if she might be shedding the virus to others, she doesn't even care to take a stab at the question. (Pun totally unintended, but I'll leave it, because we need every bit of humor we can muster right now.) Wasn't Christ all about healing the sick, caring for the vulnerable?

I shook when I read your letter, then shook again, when I watched that woman. I know what it's like to fight for breath. To fight for my daughter's breath. But it's not just the virus, of course. There's the way it's used to pad the coffers for a handful of people with enough wealth to feed, house, and provide health care for all the world. I mean, if they had a nanoparticle of a soul lodged in their flesh, they would use their resources to stop us from mainlining fossil fuels, and make enough PPE for the whole fucking world. Every day, I think I cannot be more frightened, more outraged. And then by the time I am in bed and curled up against the only man I've ever cleanly loved, I am more of all those things.

The one thing we need as much as sunlight and air right now is good sleep. We cannot fight the virus or the dangerous men in power if we're not rested so our immune systems can do their damn jobs. Say, did you know that melatonin is thought to be a frontline defense against this new illness? People are dying from cytokine storms—meaning the immune system kicks into high gear for the fight but then it turns on itself, attacking all the organs with cytokines, whatever those are. I imagine little cyclones careening through our bodies, another freak weather disaster brought to you by the makers of climate collapse. Melatonin weakens the cytokine storms, and so my naturopath says take some and keep taking it until this whole damn thing blows over.

But will it ever be over? The virus is exacting a toll as if it's bred for Trump's bidding. This week, the virus killed twenty people in the Navajo Nation, while the entire state of New Mexico, with thirteen times more residents, lost only sixteen. An Asian American nurse who was ferrying medicine to a patient was spat on. Black people are dying in far greater numbers than whites, even as they are kicked out of stores for wearing masks that make them somehow look suspicious when they are just trying to buy food for their families. Imagine, one of those masked Black men being escorted outside as the blood-covered, mask-less, white woman prances in.

The epilepsy community has a poster child for the "Charlotte's Web" strain of CBD, which was developed to bring young Charlotte Figi's seizures safely to heel. She lived here in Colorado, and after a serious illness that was treated as COVID-19 triggered a seizure, Charlotte died of respiratory failure and cardiac arrest. She was thirteen, and had thrived on CBD for several years. In this pandemic, parents of epileptics are terrified for our still-seizing kids. Weekly I search for Ruby's meds the way you searched for your passport—I have had to call other states because sometimes I can't find her meds locally. I saw a notice today, urging Norwegian students studying abroad to return home: "This applies especially if you are staying in a country with poorly developed health services and infrastructure and/or collective infrastructure, for example, the USA." I, too, think Canada is looking pretty good.

We sound like handmaids, plotting to flee Gilead. Meanwhile, most of my neighbors and family are more of the mind to take a stand, with guns. They see this president as someone who is fighting to take back something they lost, or fear losing. I have broken my neck trying to understand it but even as I love a subset of Trump supporters, even as I want the best for their farms and businesses and families, I don't believe this president who grabs women by the pussy and brags about it, who has gutted every law that protects our food, air, land, and water, really gives a damn about any of them, either. And as he pits us against one another, our basic needs are slipping through our highly sanitized fingers.

Now I am wondering about your finger again. Is it healing?

And now I am wondering about healing generally. Can we ever? Here, in America? It's hard to imagine, when even old friends with whom you've been in the trenches to protect the places you love with all the dark red meaty marrow in your bones, find it sporting to put down women over a holiday meal.

To be clear, I did speak up—although I wanted to throw the turkey and all the trimmings into their laps. I hated for my daughter to think that's what a good, balanced conversation among equals looks like because it's not. Sadly, in these situations—and no doubt you know this—the more angry and upset I get, the more they say well, the poor dear. It's clear she's bought a one-way ticket on the crazy train.

One of the guys, a vegan, turned his nose up at much of the dinner despite a good deal of non-animal fare. He didn't bring food or offer to help with dishes or even clear his plate. He never said thank you. What he did say—when I was talking about the ancient badass women warriors—was that he found my thesis "uninteresting."

This is how I land in my father's house: when the gaslighting is so deft I don't see it coming. Meaning I can see Trump's brash, crude version a mile away. It is much harder to see it in men like my father, who are well-spoken. My dad loved Beethoven's 9th on Sunday morning, "The Cremation of Sam McGee" for a bedtime story. He was a man who loved the wild world so much that it brought him to tears when we spotted a moose, or a family of quail. He wanted me to love these things, and he seemed to think I was worthy of being introduced to them. And yet he touched my body, commented on my body, in all the wrong ways, ways that made me want to die in my skin.

It still catches me off guard. I'll be working with men that care about restoring the lynx population only to find out that they still don't care about women. The bad dinner conversation caused Devin much anguish because he didn't know these guys and he was trying to figure out if this was just the kind of debate that hardcore activists had during the holidays (in which case, he wasn't sure he wanted to be a part of it again), or if they were really as set on undermining me as it appeared. I think it took us both some time to figure out that they were the gold medallion level gaslighters. These are the sophisticated, educated, and nuanced version of misogyny—the kind that sits on the left side of the congressional aisle and says all the right things but in the end it's the same thing as the guys on the right: they'll protect their access to power because they truly believe they are superior. At the end of the day, those aren't the kind of guys I want in the foxhole because they'll never really have our backs.

This is not to say there aren't good, decent men out there, and this year I am more wildly grateful to them than I have ever been in all the years of my life combined. You can single them out because they will be the only ones who won't get their dander up about these letters. Instead they will read in earnest, then look right at you, and with humility say, "Hey, wow, so that's how it is for you. My god, I'm sorry. And enraged. Tell me how I can best help."

Remember the recent shakedown in the Grand Canyon, over female river guides getting harassed and even assaulted? A very reliable friend confirmed what he had seen, during his days on the river. How young women were hazed as though they were freshmen going through a fraternity's rush week—intimidated into humiliating sex acts just to get a summer job, a job that should be the most exhilarating and empowering experience in their young lives. Those same guys are likely going to vote the same ticket we'll be voting in November, that is, if there's an election. And I don't know what to do with that.

I'm glad you know that there is no time to prove your worthiness by making things more of a challenge than they are. Not anymore. That's what they want: for your body to be so weak and exhausted that you cannot fight back. So many studies show that women do far more paid and unpaid labor, that they are far less able to take personal time, or sick leave. Sleep and self-care must be our first lines of defense. This matters whether you are a doctor, a teacher, a UPS driver, a mother. This matters too if you are a writer. The writing that comes from that deep place can only be accessed when we're not in fight-or-flight. We need to crawl in the bear den not so much to give birth but to dream away the darkness. We need that insular time in the underworld, where our bodies tangle with taproots and our stories churn in the soil.

I dreamed last night about a snake that had its skin peeled away. It was raw pink flesh, and it was writhing in terror and agony, as if the world were too much to bear without that barrier. Whatever masochisms and projections we have harbored, we must peel them away—but we need our hides, our scales and feathers. We need our fangs and claws. We need razor-sharp perceptions and reflexes. A snake's infrared sensory system is a good metaphor, too. To help us feel our way out of the father's house—but not before we set the place on fire and watch the motherfucker burn. We can't wait to find out that the conversation isn't just dinner party talk, that passports aren't being issued due to health and safety concerns but for much more sinister reasons. At this point, we must assume the worst, and then throw all our weight into that fight. The fight for our lives. For the lives of the daughters we did or did not have.

But there's this, too: yesterday, Craig, his fiancé Daiva, Devin, and I slipped into a canyon out in the west end of the county, a canyon with big bear tracks in cool damp mud—the animal so recently departed we could still smell her dank fur—a commingling of mud, sex, carrion. A bear who had just emerged from her den, clear-eyed and rested. At the canyon head, a single pool quivering with tiny, wriggling bits of life. The cottonwood trees, about to leaf out in vivid candy color—Jolly Rancher green apple. My mouth watered, just looking at them.

From my side of the mountains to yours,
Amy

Hi Amy,

I watched a woman's husband die last night in real time on Twitter. It was no one I knew.

She tweeted: *They took him to the hospital, they had the breathing thing attached and doing chest compressions. I can't go with him.*

Then she tweeted: *He's too young for this, I'm supposed to go first* (though in her picture she looked quite young).

Then she tweeted: *I can do NOTHING here I can't do anything. They'll call me. What can I do. I can't go to the hospital.*

And then: *I just don't know what to do.*

And then: *He's died they couldn't bring him back.*

And then Leah M, a person I only know from Twitter, a person I follow because she is smart about politics, tweeted back: *Lisa, we don't know each other, but I have 20 years experience as a therapist. If you want to talk, I just followed you so you can DM me. I'll be up until at least midnight. (No charge, of course. Just two humans connecting.)*

And then: *Can you drink something with sugar in it? Some tea or juice? And make sure you are warm enough? Put on a hoodie or put a fluffy blanket around your shoulders?*

And then: *And please remember to take deep belly breaths. Inhale fully through your nose, letting your belly expand, and exhaling through gently pursed lips. If your hands or other extremities start to tingle or feel numb, sit or lie down, okay?*

This is what tenderness looks like in the world we have made. Reminding one another to breathe.

I don't know how it happened, or who I am connected to, but Charlotte Figi's death showed up in my Facebook feed and of course I thought of Ruby first and you, and hoped somehow that news would miss you, which I see now was a dumb thing to hope for. I did not realize Charlotte was in Colorado, but of course you would know about her wherever she was. I'm sorry about so many things, but I'm sorry above all there is that extra fear for you, which is no doubt accelerated by Charlotte's story. Did you guys ever get your test results from the county? Do you know if you have antibodies?

When you go hiking with Craig and Daiva do you stay six feet apart from each other, or are you all "family" enough that you aren't distancing? Here people are really afraid, partly because they closed all the clinics within three counties.

Everyone is masked now, in town. At the post office we do what the post mistress calls the do-si-do, because we step up and put the package down and then step way back, and then she steps forward and weighs the package, and then steps way back, and then we put our credit card in and retreat, and then she pushes buttons on her side. All of this plus a giant sheet of plexiglass between us. Not that I am casting aspersions. If I had her job I would probably be out of my mind with sitting-duck fear. I'm just saying, people are scared. No one is being social at all. If we cross paths on a trail with friends or strangers, nobody touches anybody's dogs.

Mike and I went back to that new trail this evening. This is the only time it will be viable because it is snow-covered all winter and the cows own it from mid-May till September, but right now it is heaven. There are at least twenty nesting pairs of bluebirds along one hundred yards of creek. It's wind-protected and alive with robins and mallards and geese, and some little bird that looks like a towhee, but I think is too small to be one (have to look it up). I listened hard for the rattle of a belted kingfisher. All my life she's been my "everything's going to be okay after all" sighting, uncanny in her ability to show up just when I fear all hope is lost. But there was not sight nor sound of her today along that creek full of birds, which either means all hope is not lost yet, or else everything is *not* going to be okay.

On the way home in the car we passed the herd of Rocky Mountain bighorn who live upriver. Tons of lambs this season. They are having trouble keeping those babies alive beyond a year, and there's a lot of discussion about the (barely) domesticated sheep the Basque shepherds run through here along the Central Stock Driveway every summer infecting them. But the herd couldn't look healthier right now. Around the big bend in the Rio Grande we saw about one hundred elk, and watched from at least a mile away, as they leapt the fence one by one on their way back up the mountain.

When they all got over, we proceeded, but as we passed the place where they had crossed we saw that a yearling cow had gotten two legs twisted in the fence. We both got out and tried to pull the fence but her legs were locked down tight, three strands wrapped around two legs and each other—the worst twist there is—so we raced to the house (about ten minutes, downriver to the bridge and then back up the other side), threw the dogs inside, grabbed the wire cutters, and raced back. The whole way back, going way too fast on the gravel road, I was thinking, she can't die, she can't cut her legs all the way through, we cannot be having COVID, and Trump selling off the North Fork, and drilling the fucking Arctic, and the cyanide bombs, and states needing to send local police to make sure the federal government does not seize the PPE they bought from China for their frontline workers, AND, AND, AND a dead yearling elk. And who knows if it was *our* fault for pulling over to watch them cross. We were far away, but still, maybe this yearling cow smelled the dogs in the car and it was enough to make her lose her concentration. What I am trying to say is that the elk became everything, it was all twenty-one thousand COVID victims, it was the Twitter lady's dead husband, it was the post office and the 2020 election, but most of all it was a yearling elk who ought not to have to jump over barbed wire fences as tall as she is just to get a fucking drink of water, one more scourge we have brought down upon the American West.

And then we were back, and I was bracing myself for her having, in our absence, cut her tendons all the way through, or deep enough that she wouldn't be able to walk when we cut her down. We looked and looked and she just wasn't there. We drove up and down twice and saw no cut fence. We got out and walked, and I found the place she'd been, the scuff marks her body had made when she was hanging, and the fence was torqued a little but not cut anywhere. We had not been gone twenty minutes—there are hardly any cars on the road right now—and I could see across the river to the spot where she was nearly the whole time we were driving. But we *had* passed one car right after we left her, and there would have been three or four minutes when the guy in that car could have set her free before we could see across the river again. Maybe he was a cowboy so fluent in barbed wire fences he knew some magic trick to get those legs out, but with Mike and I both trying we couldn't budge it. Or maybe the elk somehow kicked out on her own, which seems even more impossible given how tight those legs were wrapped.

My first thought when we couldn't find her was that she had been a ghost of the elk who had lost her life in *my* barbed wire four or five years ago at the ranch, or some other spirit thing, an omen, a sign, a girl elk come to tell me Trump is about to start jailing women who speak out against him, maybe as early as next week, and it's time to make for Canada and take a walk through that border-land forest. When I found the spot where she'd been, not a speck of blood anywhere, I thought it might be a sign of a different kind, that somehow this virus *will* change hearts and minds and the way we walk on the Earth and what kind of person we want to be president. Maybe the female kind. Maybe against all odds the wild Earth will escape.

After all, what single thing could be better designed than this virus to show us what me-ism gone mad in America has wrought? How desperately unprepared we are on every level to fight it, to keep people alive, to keep people sheltered, to offer people the safety net citizens of most civilized countries take for granted. The best science fiction writer in the world could not have invented anything more demonstrative of the depth and breadth of our government's colossal failure.

And yet in spite of the current regime's determination to create a society where no one is interested in helping each other, look at so many of us staying at home, making masks, making the right choice no matter how hard they have tried to beat it out of us. Imagine if we had a leader who could harness all that good will instead of one who mocks it. Imagine living in one of the countries run by women, New Zealand, Finland, Iceland, Denmark…all of them flattening the curve and feeding their citizens. In Canada it takes two minutes online to apply for "I lost my job because of COVID" relief, and the check shows up in three days.

Maybe that teenage girl elk came along this afternoon to remind me about stamina. Self-care, sleep, osha, ginger, and garlic (I ordered melatonin yesterday), and my diffuser, which I would have been embarrassed to even mention in the time before this time (speaking of privilege) pumping out vapors of eucalyptus and hyssop and Ravensara. Maybe the elk was here to say *I know you think you are doomed, but if you kick just right you can be free again.* What does it mean to kick just right? To upend a plate full of turkey and stuffing into a misogynist's lap? To point-blank *ask* the men in our lives if it's okay with them how Trump speaks to women reporters, how Trump speaks about all women, if they are cool with the fact that America can't find nine individuals to sit on the Supreme Court who haven't raped anybody? Or does to kick just right mean to monkey-wrench, to fill the streets (will we ever again fill the streets)? Or is it time, for real, to start a revolution? And if we did start one, how to keep dudes like your Thanksgiving friends from railroading it, and making it all about their egos?

I was at a writer thing in Aspen nearly a decade ago, being taken out for expensive sushi (confession: I will do almost anything for expensive sushi), and there was a recent Pulitzer Prize winner there, and another male writer fawning all over him, and after some time the fawning man remembered I was at the table (I actually can't remember who the fawner was, but memory suggests it was someone I know a little bit) and he said to the recent Pulitzer Prize winner, have you read Pam's new book (which at the time was *Contents May Have Shifted*) and the recent Pulitzer Prize winner, who, by the way, no one had ever heard of until he came out of nowhere to win the Pulitzer Prize, smiled broadly and said, "Oh, no, I don't actually *read* books by women." And the terrible terrible thing I must confess to you now is that I didn't say one single thing. I just went back to eating my sushi. And that makes me hope our girl elk kicked her way out of the fence somehow without the help of a burly cowboy. And it makes me think we need a plan, and a good one.

Happy Easter, whatever that means.

Pam

PS Hand is nearly healed.
PPS I want you in my battalion.

Hi there Pam,

Oh, where do I begin? You wrote just forty-eight hours ago and already there is much more to say. Ruby and I watched *Tiger King*—a reality TV show about a reality not based in reality—which is exactly what we are living. There are other shows that do the same thing: *Duck Dynasty*, *Keeping Up With the Kardashians*, *Naked and Afraid*. But in this one, the dark workings of unacknowledged trauma are so apparent. The way it gets projected squarely onto women and tigers says it all.

So I know exactly what you mean about that young she-elk being everything. Oh, that younger you—not saying anything to the mean Pulitzer Prize winner. The fantasy I'm having is one where we pack his nasal cavities with wasabi.

Then there's a younger me who at nineteen flew to NYC with my mom's then-boyfriend, a seemingly good guy who had gotten me an interview with Air France for a position as a ski resort liaison of sorts, for American skiers visiting the

French Alps. The job was to meet the Americans in the Lyon airport and take them via chartered bus to Courchevel, where I, if hired, would get them settled in their hotels and chalets, help them book ski lessons, meet them for dinner. I didn't know much French save what I'd learned in high school. But I hired a tutor, practiced my tail off for weeks. Slept with a French conversational cassette playing all night long, next to my bed. I wanted that job more than I'd ever wanted anything. And when I made it through the first interview in Park City, my hometown, this boyfriend of my mother's, my connection to the airline, accompanied me to the New York offices for a second interview. When we arrived, we were informed there was no hotel room, that we'd be staying in the apartment belonging to the American man who had interviewed me in Park City. First, we went out for—you guessed it—expensive sushi. I remember drinking enough sake that I challenged the sushi chef, who was a former sumo wrestler, to an arm wrestle. He won, of course.

Later, in the apartment that turned out to be a studio apartment, the guy gave my mom's boyfriend and me the foldout couch—which was awkward but there was so little real estate it was hard to sleep anywhere else. Our host took the floor. I woke up in the middle of the night to find him on top of me, and then I was wrestling for real, but weirdly, I wrestled in silence—because, get this, I didn't want to wake up my mom's boyfriend. Of course, there is no way that he slept through the whole thing, but he pretended to. On my own, I fended the guy off, but just barely. For the rest of the night I didn't sleep for a single minute. I lay there wide-eyed, my body coiled like a box spring.

I didn't even get that it was an attack. That my mother's boyfriend had let me be assaulted. All I know is, the next day, my head was wrapped in wet wool as I sat down in one of the fancy Air France offices with the VP of Marketing. I bumbled my way through the interview. Eventually, the VP said, "Your French is an atrocity, but you're cute enough. You've got the job." I was so grateful. Grateful!

My mom's boyfriend never said a word about the night at the apartment. And then the guy who had climbed on top of me and said, "You owe me," set out to make my winter in the Alps miserable. He even tried to get me fired—but I at least knew how to fight back in that arena. Meaning I kept my job. It was one of the best winters the Alps had ever seen—I mean, fresh, shoulder-high powder almost every morning for two months. It took me years to see why I failed to savor it, why I stayed holed up in my little apartment eating croissants except when I was on duty, helping American tourists. Here's the kicker, though. It wasn't until *last year* at fifty-three years of age that I recalled the night in the apartment and could name it for what it was. I told my mother about it, and her response was vague. I'm guessing it was hard for her to hear because she, like so many of us, has been caught in that kind of fence, tongue and body tangled, more than once in her life.

You asked about the countywide testing for COVID-19 antibodies. Unfortunately, the tests were delayed because the testing lab is in NY and a) they're having a hard time getting the blood samples there due to breaks in the transportation chain; and b) they can't get workers into the lab because they are all home sick with the very virus they were hired to test for. There's also some rift between the county health folks and the owners of the biotech company. They are no longer putting out joint press releases, and the separate releases often have contradictory statements. So this hopeful effort seems to have fallen apart. Very few of us know if we have antibodies, or if we should be more aggressively quarantined. The way this played out has been affirming for the folks who believed the whole thing was too Big Brother.

The other day, we were buying some beer to enjoy on separate tailgates after our hike with

Craig and Daiva (we do take two cars, and we do keep ourselves far apart from one another while walking). A big black pickup, one with a MAGA sticker, pulled up in front of the liquor store. It was a man I know, a man who I am a little afraid of but also like—if that isn't fucked up right out of the starting gate.

So here's my newest dirty secret, and I feel so ashamed, that even here and now, I let myself be caught in the wires again: I was beside my car, having just put beer in the cooler when this guy strode over with open arms. I froze. It happened so fast, but I let him hug me. I held my breath, I barely hugged back, but I let him hug me. It was an instant and then I jumped back, and said it was nice to see him, but we shouldn't be hugging. He scowled and said it was clear neither of us was sick. But I *was* sick. Sick that I froze, that I let him tangle with me. Not only was I that girl-elk, but he was my father, he was the Air France guy, he was my ex-lovers, he was the guys at Thanksgiving, he was Trump and Kavanaugh. He was the hunter and I was the hunted and in that moment I could only play my prescribed part in that equation. I want to puke now, telling you about it. My heart was pounding when I got in the car and grabbed the wipes (the only ones we have), and scrubbed myself silly. Then I had Devin scrub my back, where the man's hands touched my shoulders. As if I could scrub away that equation, that agreement. As if I could start over, and just say NO. The whole thing made me think that maybe I have no business writing a book about being like badass women warriors.

I have to keep looking beyond the fence, to the horizon, to know there is more out there, that I have every reason to keep kicking. I was ready to give up yesterday and just then, there was the good news from the Wisconsin election—the more fair-minded female judge who unseated one of the less fair incumbents and this was despite all but 5 of 180 voting precincts remaining open statewide. And Bernie's endorsement of Biden. I watched their conversation/speech this morning and while I am so angry because Elizabeth Warren really deserved to be endorsed by these two old white guys, I am glad to know that there is authentic unity happening, that we are still capable of that.

But before the election, we have a postal service to save, don't we? Or we'll just have to drive folks to the polls, even if we do it gloved and masked and the car windows wide open in an early winter storm.

Which brings me to the hardest thing—or maybe it's all the hardest thing, now. I refer to the death on Twitter, to which you bore witness. Losing someone to the coronavirus is a lot like losing someone to adventure: they go up a mountain, or down a river, and there is an accident. You might never get to say goodbye. You might never get to see their body. The difference is, COVID-19 patients don't die doing what they loved.

So we must be careful. Out in the wild, in the kitchen. At the same time, let us hope that we continue to live in a world where we can still die doing what we love—whether it's walking in wilderness or chopping vegetables. Let's hope that the only way out is not alone in an ICU, where our bodies get tricked into attacking our own lungs. Let's hope we can hold on to that kind of freedom—in the high country, in the canyons. That we can watch the elk clear the fence, the horned toads scurry over stone. That we can be more than hunted. That we can fuck up by staying silent, by not saying no—but then have the chance to say NO the next time, and be heard.

Devotedly, from within the battalion,

Amy

Hey Amy,

I love all your letters, but I might love this last one most of all.

A lamb was born here today, to my old matriarch, Jordan. It is late for lambs, and I only have two ewes left after a 350-pound black bear came down the mountain a couple of years ago and decimated my herd, and I would have thought Jordan might be done. She's eight if she's a day and maybe nine or ten. But when I went out to feed this morning, she had that look in her eye, pushing out little Lamaze breaths, and so I separated her into the horse stall and left her alone (which is what she prefers) and came inside and finished Rebecca Solnit's book about feminism and hope. Two hours later the lamb was already up and nursing, a dark brown color with the tightest little curls imaginable. I wanted to leave them alone today, but fingers crossed it is a little ewe. We have two rams here at the moment, and two is already one too many.

As I watched the days in April tick by, I thought maybe we weren't going to have any lambs this year, that my surviving ewes were too old and too traumatized. I was okay with it, I mean, don't we have enough going on without worrying whether an aging ewe has enough milk to sustain a lamb? Or whether the smell of her udder is enough to bring another bear down the mountain to stalk us? But when I made eye contact with Jordan this morning in her semi-distress (she's such an old hand at this) I realized I had been wrong to hope for the easy way out, and new life is new life. If there was ever a year I can attend to the needs of my Icelandics it's this one, and I imagine Elsie will drop here in a week or two and by the looks of her belly (now that I'm no longer in denial) she probably has twins.

Plus, if we are in need of metaphors, there are no ewes tougher than Icelandic ewes. Ask any shearer that question and they will confirm. Jordan, in fact, fought the black bear with her head in his mouth for some period of time, because the morning after the massacre she had four holes in her neck, one you could have put a corn cob inside of. (The ewes and lambs were inside; the bear ripped the barn door right off its hinges.) She got stitched up, we gave her shots every day for a month, and she came through. She stomps her little hooves hard at the dogs, and all her life has nursed the orphans. She watched that bear kill generations of her babies two years ago, and here she is, persisting through the pandemic.

I love the story about the dude in the black truck, in part because it so easily could have happened to me, and I would have been stripping in the car and lighting my clothes on fire in the front yard when I got home, and maybe not even realizing it wasn't fear of the disease making me do it.

You have every right to write about the ferocity of women, more right than some writer (if there is such a person) who is so sure of herself she responds correctly every time. Rebecca Solnit's new book is about how we grew up in a culture where violence toward women, where stories of women's erasure, were so common, whether we were personally abused or not, whether we were raped or not, whether we were cut up into little pieces and shoved into the back of someone's refrigerator. The fact it *was* happening two blocks or two miles or two states away almost continuously, made us less confident, less free, less able to say, automatically, don't you fucking touch me, when someone tries to hug us at a liquor store during a pandemic.

But you and I, each in our own way, grew up in your father's duck blind. We thought because we could make the boys forget we were girls and keep up with them on the double black diamonds and rock faces, we had circumvented the kind of danger those urban girls ran into when they walked home from work on the streets of San Francisco. But we were still trained to please those men, to feed their egos, to let them instruct us in the proper way of wrapping our oars in duct tape even though we had been on the river for ten years and it was their very first season.

That guy hugging you makes me want to shriek so loud you could hear it on the other side of the San Juan Range, but would I have shrieked if it had been me he hugged? Also, his hugging is so loaded in so many different ways—a flirt, a test, a political assertion—it makes me want to take a shower.

The bear that put Jordan's head in his mouth stalked us for more than a month after the first massacre, and I slept with my windows open and went charging out there with the shotgun the fish and game warden loaned me every time I heard a noise. I'd boarded up the broken door by then, and one night, as I ran screaming for the barn barefoot in my nightshirt, the bear came flying out a newly broken window at me, gave me one long look, and galloped up the hillside in the other direction. He didn't kill anybody that night—I caught him in time—but thinking now of those nights I ran straight at him make me realize how much I would rather die by 350-pound black bear, or canyoneering accident, or lightning, or great white shark, than by a hug from a guy with a MAGA sticker.

You have no doubt, by now, seen Josh Bickel's photograph from the *Columbus Dispatch* (which ought to win a Pulitzer), the zombie apocalypse photo of the Trumpees clawing at the window of the Ohio statehouse, protesting social distancing, and of course, breathing and spitting and panting all over each other in the process. So much for the goodness of the citizenry. When I saw it, and the Michigan protest, saw, specifically, a MAGA-hatted young man purposely blow in the face of the masked reporter on-site, I kind of startled awake and thought, oh, the Civil War is actually underway now (or maybe it has been for years) but instead of shooting each other, we are breathing on each other, and here we are, back around again, to the breath.

I think we are going to be home for a long time. (Since national and local testing wasn't financially profitable.) And I think the longer we are home the more hope there is the world will change in giant ways. I know those will be hard changes, because so many will be desperately poor and many others will die, perhaps us among them.

But will there ever be a better case made for a Green New Deal? Could trickledown economics finally die the death that's been waiting for it for three decades?

I read an article today suggesting that the people who are dying so furiously from COVID may be dying because of their exposure to Roundup. That Roundup is in our gas tanks in the form of ethanol, and so people who live near highways are dying more, harder and faster than people who don't. This correlates with other studies that show places with bad air see a 25 percent higher mortality rate from COVID, and the reason may be one chemical or a hundred chemicals, but after I finished the article, I thought, if we have known one damn thing for decades it's that Roundup kills people. How fucked up are we that we would rather be dead than have weeds?

A friend who works (kind of against his will) in a sporting goods store told me last night that when people come in to buy guns and they have to run background checks there are usually, on average, about fifty background checks in the system at one time, and in the weeks right before and right after the shelter-in-place order went into effect that number went to thirteen thousand. I don't know whether that's nationally, or statewide, or for this particular chain of stores, but whatever it is, the ratio is the point. My very top priority at the moment is not to let Trump kill me, and I believe that extends to anyone wearing a MAGA hat and/or camo. And by kill, I mean shoot me or breathe on me. I know that's not a very altruistic or even useful goal, but all the useful shit I might do during or after the pandemic is predicated on me staying alive.

Do I believe Trump is my father returned from the dead to kill me? I wish I could qualify my yes somehow, but all qualifications sound like a lie. I'd rather take one of my own Wüsthof cooking knives to the breast or swan dive off Muley Point than let one of those motherfuckers in the *Columbus Dispatch* photo breathe on me. I know I am supposed to have compassion for their desperation, but I spent that compassion years ago. Which might mean I am ready for battle. "The death of a beautiful woman is, unquestionably, the most poetical topic in the world," said Edgar Allan Poe, via Rebecca Solnit, who notes, "He must not have imagined it from the perspective of women who prefer to live."

I've ridden those Mongolian horses, and I like their spirit. I followed the Przewalski horses for miles across the steppes with my camera and I liked them too. The Icelandic horses are not unlike those Mongolians, compact, tough, generous, sure-footed. Maybe the horses are more than a metaphor. Maybe they are actual horses. Like the ones who saved you after Ruby was born. Maybe this is what the West was made for, a place where horses and women can work in tandem to smash gender roles and overturn the patriarchy, the oligarchy, ban Roundup forever, make gaslighting a crime that carries with it twenty-five years in prison, rename all the rivers and buildings and national parks after grocery store clerks and ICU nurses and UPS drivers. Maybe the world has been waiting for horses and women to team up again, like they did way back when in Mongolia.

When I am on the back of a horse I trust, I feel its determination and courage rise right up through me. It would not be the worst way to go, to be shot off the back of a large-hearted horse.

It must be late, if my fantasies have turned to actual, if somewhat archaic, war death, so that means I should stop. There is a way to fight this madness and a way to win. And life with my father made me into someone who belongs on the front line. I just have to figure out the morality of it, the best way to do it, which I think is at the heart of these conversations.

Hope you are well over there. It is morning now and looks like it's going to be a pretty one.

Going to go out and check on Jordan and the lamb, whom we have named Becky.

Love to you from this side,
Pam

April 17, 2020

Hey Pam,

*And this, in turn, is my favor-
ite letter from you.* Which I think
means we are building momentum,
or muscle—or maybe it means that
we've summoned the steppe women on
the steppe horses and they are now thundering through our words, our veins. I say perfect
timing. I say this as I look out across that hulking
mass known as the Uncompahgre Plateau—the
most solid thing that comes between our two high
country homes—as silver curtains drop rain that
never touches, that moves on these southwesterly
springtime winds from my topography to yours.

The photo you sent, of Jordan and her lamb,
says it all. About survival. About what is female
and what endures. Our female animals have taught
us to be bold and enduring. That's what scared
Edgar Allan Poe—who my father also read to me
at bedtime. The stamina we have.

More men are dying of this new virus, and
that is not just because they smoke more and go
to the doctor less, it's also because they have an

X and a Y chromosome and the immune system adaptations come from the X, which we have two of. In other words, if the bag of tricks they've got in their X don't help them survive, the Y doesn't provide alternatives. But if our first bag of X tricks fails, we have a whole new bag to turn to, for options. Literally, we are more capable of enduring.

That said, in the case of our goats, the one female didn't fare so well as the males. We had male pack goats, one of which Ruby rode when we went hiking, but we also had a little Nubian Ruby named Dora the Explorer, who was going to be a milk goat. She was dainty and goofy (what goat isn't goofy?) and she was killed by a bear that in turn went after Ruby's dad when he went outside to see what the commotion was about. Herb ran to the shed for a gun and the bear climbed out of the pen and cornered Herb on the threshold while poor Dora screamed in the background. Herb ran for the door and shoved the bear back outside. (The rake marks from his claws still mar the threshold.) The bear sauntered into the trees, but as soon as Herb came back out and tried to get to Dora, the bear came at him again. Herb and our three dogs were forced to play a cat and mouse game for an hour before they finally made a run for the house. Once inside they shut the door, and there was the bear with his nose to the glass, trying to get in. Later we buried Dora and put a huge stone slab over her, but the bear came back and shoved the damn thing aside, dug her up from four feet down, and dragged her off. Ruby and I weren't there that night—as usual, we were at a hospital in a big city, but still she had bad bear dreams for a time. As you can imagine. What was cool was how the dreams of "bad" bears (as if there's such a thing) eventually became Winnie-the-Poohs. Not that we want to reduce wild animals to cartoon characters, but here's evidence that our minds can heal hatred!

I hesitate to line it up so that female equals life and endurance and male equals death and destruction but in the few hours between our letters, the White House has weakened limits of mercury and other toxic pollutants for oil and coal-fired power plants. Meanwhile, I've got guys who want "to connect with me" on Messenger who feel they can say whatever they want about my looks, my writing, and then get pissed when I'm not flattered. I block them of course, immediately, but how is it that, now that they are home and unemployed, they have all this time and expect me to somehow help me pass it—while objectifying myself in the process?

It's never been so clear to me, this umbilicus between misogyny and the devastation of the natural world. (Again, I don't mean all men, not at all! But why do I feel like I must keep qualifying that? Am I still somehow trying to help them feel more comfortable with what I am saying? Can't they do that emotional labor themselves?) I took all the women's studies classes at the University of Utah so I read *Women and Nature* more than once. But even that seminal work didn't quite get to the malevolence of what exists now. As a woman who likes men a great deal, who prefers much of what has been deemed a more masculine world—where mud and mountains and bringing home meat for the freezer matter more than a good haircut or a nice purse—it's hard to admit that such hatred exists. I think I blamed women for a long time, because it was easier than facing the truth, that loathing, that lock-us-up or cut-us-into-pieces thing that women feel daily in one form or another.

This afternoon, I walked with my friend who went to Mongolia with me. We went up the ridge behind the house, the sagebrush as potent as ever. The light was quicksilver. We scared up a sage grouse, a rare Gunnison type, I believe. When we got back to the house, we drank prosecco on the patio—a first, after the cold wet spring. Ruby sat with us and we were talking about the newer *Mad Max* film—the one where Charlize Theron busts out of the compound with an oil tanker full of breast milk and a handful of the last fertile ladies on Earth. I love that movie so much more than the old Mel Gibson ones—even though I loved those too. Suddenly, without any forethought, I turned to Ruby and said, "I think your placenta is buried in the bottom of your dad's freezer." Ruby's jaw hit the table and then she started howling with laughter. "Mom," she said, "you know I have to write an essay about that."

That's my girl. She endures a lot, including me. And already she's looking for tales to tell. Those she can claim as her own.

These bodies of ours. They give and they receive. They endure brutality and they conjure beauty. But mostly we are badass. Our organs, our chromosomes, our immune systems, our creative cores. We can weaponize words, we can turn oil into milk. We can re-story the world.

Joseph Campbell and all the other old white guys who dug around in ancient burials and ruins made up myths that had little to do with women. They told tales of the painted French caves as if there were only men—as shamans, as mighty hunters—who were worthy of the journey into those depths. But there's one cave, the Gargas Cave, and it is my favorite because instead of stalactites and stalagmites it's full of these subtle folds and partings. Not so long ago, they discovered, through the study of bones, that the dozens of ochre-stenciled handprints in that cave were made largely by female hands—which turns the whole mighty male hunter/shaman thing on its ear. This thrills me, because I couldn't bear the thought of women never making that journey, a half-mile underground with a single burning juniper fuse for light—such a precarious light—to sketch their own dreams and tell their own stories. But they were there. Just as we are here now, my hand pressing these keys as if I am pressing those walls, as if I am meeting your fingertips on the other side of that hulking plateau full of elk and aspen and more mountain lions than anywhere else on the planet.

Sending love downwind,
Amy

Hi Amy,

A bit of that rain made it over here from your house, and just before sunset some made it to the ground. I went out onto the porch and listened to it hit the roof and breathed and breathed it in. How many droughty summers have I stood on the porch and begged the clouds to come down from the mountains and drop a little water on my pasture. How many days during the West Fork fire did I try to make those clouds build with my mind, my will, my everything.

How many days have my laundry, my teeth, my lungs been coated with dust because the trucks hauling gravel from my neighbor's gravel pit feel the need to go sixty-five on a posted thirty-five mph gravel road, and why? Don't they get paid by the hour?

We are months, or at least weeks, from fire season, and my mind cannot even go to what that might mean during COVID, during the nightmare that is this federal government's response. More rain is forecast for tomorrow, maybe even a couple inches of snow. Every drop of moisture we get now is in the plus column, for the health of the pasture, for the health of the firefighters, for the mental health of all of us who can only lay so many disasters one on top of the other and still be able to breathe.

I didn't sleep last night because right before I went to bed, I read about our so-called attorney general saying he was going to take legal action against governors who have stringent stay-at-home orders. It's not like we haven't known all along this administration is trying to kill us, but the fact they've gone so upfront about it elevates my anxiety. The governor of Las Vegas said today that she would like her city to be a test case for dying, and when Anderson Cooper asked her whether she would go onto the casino floor every night with the workers, she hedged and hedged and then said, "Well, for one thing, I have a family."

I think a lot of us didn't know precisely what we meant when we said six or twelve or twenty-four months ago that things were going to get worse before they got better, but now we have some of the picture. The lieutenant governor of Texas saying, "Life is not the most important thing." The protestor in Tennessee, who I heard described as a man, but from the photo seems most certainly a woman, holding the sign saying, "Sacrifice the Weak, Reopen Tennessee," and the other sign from North Carolina, "Liberty or Tranny?" A sign that, if it appeared in a movie, everyone in the audience would roll their eyes. Even here, on the Creede Happenings FB page, which is supposed to be apolitical, there is talk of putting us "unpatriotic rats out of our misery." I know they hate my type, but what about the nurses? Have they no respect for fifty thousand dead?

I have taken to watching those Dodo videos where an aging pit bull is found on a sixteen-inch chain, twenty-four inches from a water dish, then hauled off by a lady wearing a sweatshirt with unicorns on it, fed first from an eye dropper, encouraged after weeks of healing to try to walk on four bandaged feet. Next thing you know the same dog is racing around a too-green backyard with three other dog friends, a man in a chair with a name like Harvey or Harry drinking a beer and laughing, and I try with all my might to believe he never hits them, never even raises his voice.

The videos always skip the long middle, the part between when you know the pitty is going to live and the part where he is racing happily around the yard as sound as the day is long. We will be that pit bull when Trump is done with us, and hallelujah for the woman in the unicorn sweatshirt who notices us in some shadeless corner of the trailer park. Or maybe we will *be* the women with the unicorn sweatshirt, looking around for one goddamn sweet thing to save.

I guess it's time to admit I'm getting really angry (ha, I am sure you were not picking up on that). I work so hard to transform my anger into direct action, every day of my life, but today there's anger left over. It is *fucking* Earth Day, and I have given money to the NRDC and the Sierra Club and the League of Conservation Voters, extra money, because I give every month, while the monster-in-chief opens up more land to drilling, and oil is worth negative $3.50 a barrel, whatever that can possibly mean.

I wish this were not the case, but I *hate* those maskless men on the Capitol steps with their AR15s, and the woman in her USA T-shirt who told the nurse in Denver to go back to China. It's not healthy to feel about them the way I do and I know it, but agreeing to disagree isn't going to cut it anymore as I watch this administration attack and destroy every single thing that brings me joy: air and water, sure, trees and animals, every slice of wildness we have left, but also the arts, education, diversity itself, Amtrak, solar power, the post office. I think about the water cannons and brutality at Standing Rock, and the fact that there were zero arrests at any of the NRA-funded protests this week and it makes my heart hurt because maybe we *are* truly beyond redemption.

Unless it is time to redefine *we*. As in, who is the we I want to be part of? Certainly not the *we* of America. Not even the *we* of Colorado, a state I love with all my heart. The *we* of the human race could be argued for, but maybe the *we* of living beings is a happier category. The *we* of horses, dogs, lambs, kingfishers, and Plymouth Barred Rock hens, the *we* of the canyon walls and the bristlecone pines, and the bluebird that comes and sits right on the top of the skinny pine tree outside my bedroom window at seven a.m. exactly and calls his bluebird call. The *we* of the people who lived sustainably in the American West for thousands of years, not that they will have us, not that we have any right to ask. The *we* of women who love the Earth and who are ready to put their minds and hearts and art and bodies on the line to defend it. More than ever before, I am that woman. There is nothing the fuck else to be now but all in.

COVID is but a coming attraction of what the climactic catastrophe has in store for us. And now we know how utterly unprepared we are to meet whatever Mother Earth might serve up when she decides once and for all to shake her most determined parasite off her back. The decision to master the Earth instead of love her was made long ago by the same sort of men who are using COVID as an excuse to steal even more from her. And yet it is hard not to notice how happy she is without us out there, how blue the sky, how shimmery the trees.

If and when we get to the other side of this pandemic, the only thing that's going to feel like *living* is fighting for the Earth, and by extension ourselves, our daughters and our "daughters," whatever percentage of people there are left who love the Earth more than money. I used to think politics was complicated, but it may be as simple as that.

Am I part of the *we* who has contributed to the death of the planet? Certainly. I have flown and flown. I use technology (thank you, Earth, for superconductors). Does that mean I have no right to speak out against the unmitigated greed of the current regime, of every regime, against oil, against dirty mining, for solar power, for a Green New Deal? No! To think so is to be gaslighted, in all the ways women have been gaslighted since the beginning of time.

Let's think for a minute about the long middle those pit bull videos skip. Let's say we have a new president. Let's say you and me, aren't, after all, dead. Let's say fifty million Americans, maybe more, are out of work, and hungry, and homeless. Let's say a little civil war breaks out after Biden is elected, and the military is doing their damndest not to take sides. Let's say there is a vaccine, and on the day after inauguration, Biden makes it so everyone can get it, even immigrants. What happens in that long middle will determine the rest of our lives, if not the rest of history. That long middle of recession, of everybody listing a little to one side with a limp and a few holes blown through them, no small amount of PTSD, all of us hesitating just a moment before we give each other a hug. How can we be our best and most useful selves in that long middle, as women, as storytellers, as mentors, as people who hold space for other people to tell their stories, as citizens of the Earth? Those are the questions that occupy me when I can't sleep and when I am walking in the mountains.

We are the ones we have been waiting for. I've had fifty-seven years of the Earth healing me, loving me, mothering me, comforting me, delighting me, giving me the words, the nouns I needed to make my books. Giving me my life. Every single good thing. No amount of service to the Earth in however many years I have left would come close to matching the gifts she has given me. The very least I can do is devote myself entirely to her salvation. If not for her sake, then for mine.

Sometimes when I am on a pasture walk, I look to the west, past The Pyramid, and Handies Peak, Sunshine Peak, the Wetterhorn, and I know our words will one day turn into action, that one day you and I will walk and ride and rise together on behalf of this wild country we love.

I guess it must be Emotional Wednesday.

Love to you from the sunrise side
of the mountains,
Pam

Hey Pam,

Today I'm in a place beyond my custom-fit anger, grief, indignation, and despair. I am disarticulated. Especially writing, because I cannot find words or story or metaphor. There are no nouns. There is no body to embody. Abstractions apply because I feel so dislocated, adrift. This is the case everywhere but in our letters.

It's like I'm sliding in sideways (I know you love baseball) to home plate and the sliding, the arriving, is perpetual. There's knowing a ball is being thrown and it may shatter my skull from behind or make the catcher's mitt before I get there, but it's all suspended, and I'm sliding and don't know that I'll ever slide safely into home base again.

I don't know any other way to write right now. I don't know how to tell a story. I don't have language—everything, everything is about breath. I am so scared, because there is a shortage of asthma inhalers, and albuterol vials for the nebulizer that Ruby and I both use when we get the bad chest cold or flu that turns into pneumonia—which we are both prone to. I have the WORST allergies—I'd never really had them, until two summers ago, when the fires were so bad. And now, I just can't breathe. The more I learn about the way this virus attacks and the people who are most susceptible to it, well, I'm a sitting duck. Then a panic attack hits me like that baseball and then the wind's knocked right out of me.

I have been a fearless activist. I've been a bold climber, ranger, firefighter. I am built for the big risks, the fights that are tooth and nail. But I've stumbled off the battlefield into the stadium and I'm mixing metaphors. I'm sliding and the ball is coming, the other team is winning, and I'm never going to arrive. I'm never going to know the score. I don't even know what game this is or who the fuck is cheering in the bleachers. Are those Atwood's handmaids I see, with the signs that say, "My Body, My Choice," cheering for me as a woman with agency over her body, her writing, her emotional well-being, her right not to be maimed, enslaved, polluted? Or are they the protesters who refuse to wear masks, who won't keep their distance, because it feels fascist when really all we're trying to do is buy time for vaccines and medical equipment to be made? Are these folks truly okay with people dying as long as we save the economy? Must these things be mutually exclusive?

I am so gutted. I cannot breathe. And when I'm able to grab a noun I'm mixing metaphors—baseball and swords.

Yesterday, the flycatchers showed up on the little balcony attached to my writing loft, as they do every spring. They like to check in, to say they're back, to remind me they're about to start nest-building. I just stood at the door and told them I was sorry. Sorry that they were nesting in a dying world. Then our favorite doe arrived early this morning; she's unmistakable, because she has droopy, floppy ears, like a hound dog. I could barely feel joy, let alone hope. I just had this weird, dissociated sense that the deer were in the wrong place, the wrong time, the wrong reality. Which is a projection, of course, of that feeling in me.

This morning I read in *The Guardian* that the virus is able to attach to particulates of air pollution—so it can travel a good distance to infect people. Imagine, if I get infected here on my mesa and I sneeze while I'm out on the balcony talking to the flycatchers and this crazy southwestern spring wind carries it all the way to your ranch while you're out on the porch breathing in the scant rain and you get sick? I'm being dramatic of course, but the point is, this virus is no flu.

I am sliding sideways and I don't even know what sport this is. But it keeps rising up, the way I need to keep writing in this space, in this context, with someone who gets on every level what it is that needs to be said here, a woman who understands on every level what is at stake now, a person who loves the world in the way it is meant to be loved: as a whole animal set free in its big, unfettered, unpoisoned habitat.

I went looking for better news than Washington offered, to counter the small groups of hateful lunatics who have been hogging all the airtime. In our own state, police are looking for a man who went into a market in Evergreen and breathed all over the produce. I can't walk back the video footage in my head and only now that I'm writing to you about it do I realize it's the damn breathing thing again. And then we have some creepy guys who leered at Ruby when we went walking. A while back, I looked at the county sex offender site and sure enough, we have like four of them on the mesa and at least one is registered for having sexually assaulted a child. So doors are locked. Blinds get drawn. If anyone invaded, Devin and I are both pretty good with a gun, but that's not the way I want to go about my business.

Now Ruby's on third base and I have to decide whether to urge her to run for home plate, too.

She's already so scared. Angry that her childhood was stolen by illness. And now, her teen years have been hijacked by the double-whammy of climate catastrophes and a pandemic. She turns sweet sixteen in September; she had her whole party planned out. She is also sick of school on Zoom and scared that she might die like Charlotte. Fire season is almost here and she is terrified of fire, ever since the time she was little and we almost evacuated when flames came up out of the canyon, leapfrogging at our house at sixty mph. I called my neighbor that day; she was hosing down hay bales and turning the horses into the farthest pasture. She said she'd come help me load animals if it came to it. Fortunately, the wind changed. But Ruby's lived in fear since.

Oh, the fires. We don't have much time 'til they're here and what does that look like, with these relentless winds and perhaps sick firefighters and what will amount to little federal funding amid one of the worst droughts the Southwest has ever endured?

I'm sorry. I'm not too inspiring today. This is the lowest of low, this place we're in—what dystopia really looks like. How many people will be homeless and hungry and without health care? How many animals will be starved, or abandoned? I think about the books I haven't written, and now may never get to. I think about all that I wished for Ruby that didn't happen. I think of how little time I might have with the man I've only known for five years and love beyond all measure. I suspect I'll die of global heartbreak paid for by patriarchy or else I'll die from this virus—which are really one and the same. Who knew we'd be choosing from such stark options.

And yet. (Thank god, for those two words, side by side.) I have this time with you. The deer are here and out of the blue, my mother is shipping me lavender plants to put on the new patio that Devin just built—plants that she swears are deer-proof. I am holding my students' feet to the flames, and they are producing some damn good writing in the process. Ruby is pretty stable right now, and that means I am sleeping, which means that whatever I'm sliding into, whatever swords I've got in the fire are being forged anew. Someday soon I'll wield them again because this is all there is now. The battle to just *be*.

> **Onward, with love,**
> **Amy**

Dear Amy,

I think we have to take turns with our days of devastation. It is the only way we will get through. It is how women have always gotten through. Going to look for good news on the internet is not a good strategy right now, unless you go back to the rescued dogs.

William Barr threatened again today to take legal action against states with strict stay-at-home orders. Why does this one slay me more than so many others? Maybe because if there was one thing I could never reveal to my father it was that I had found a strategy to afford myself some tiny measure of protection—an afterschool class, a friend's parent who I could tell "had their eye on me" (in a good way). If said protection got revealed to my father somehow, the punishment became worse than it would have been had I left myself wide open.

I did a Zoom conversation last night with Joe Wilkins and Luis Urrea about Joe's novel, *Fall Back Down When I Die*. Mind you, these are both relatively conscious, sensitive men. Joe's novel is, on the one hand, an old-fashioned Western, with lots of good old boys running around the forest shooting each other and wolves (the novel's climax occurs during the first legal gray wolf hunt in Montana) and, on the other hand, a successful attempt to humanize (some) of those government-hating, gun-loving white dudes who were raised out in Eastern Montana by brutal and violent fathers who were raised by brutal and violent fathers who were raised by...you get the drift. I blurbed the book two years ago, when it was in galley, because it is beautifully written and because it did, in fact, make me feel empathy for the protagonist, Wendell. Wendell grew up with every disadvantage (except the big one), and over the course of the book gains a conscience, and therefore has to die. It is an old story, intelligently and sensitively updated.

I spent a few hours yesterday reacquainting myself with the book, and in the penultimate scene where the gun-toting bad men are chasing the gun-toting redeemed man (Wendell) who has his nephew, whom he loves like a son, and his love interest, Maddie, in tow, he decides they should split up so he can distract the killers and the woman and little boy can get away.

Then there is this paragraph: "She nodded and asked where, and he pointed north along the ridge, had her sight along his arm. He made sure she knew what was west, what was east, and to keep herself north, ever north. If she stayed true, he said, and kept the North Star in front of her...."

I know I don't have to go on for you to catch my drift. And I can't quite remember now whether Maddie grew up in that wild country, or how well her backstory would have allowed her to know it. But most of my women friends, and I am betting yours too, know how to find and follow the fucking North Star. I don't believe there has ever been a study proving a Y chromosome makes one more able to find one's way across a landscape after dark.

My point is not to criticize this good novel, nor to make Joe Wilkins, who is anything but the problem, into one. I do seem to be done, however, with this particular mythology where men who know the wilderness so much better than women, go out and die in it that the woman might live. That's a pretty story, but the real story of the American West, the one we have been living all our lives, is the bottomless insecurity that leads men to tame and destroy the wilderness, and now millions will die from living downwind from that destruction. We have to fess up to participating in that story before we can write a new one, and this John Wayne shit has to be the first thing to go. I realize this is what *Desert Cabal* is exactly about.

Weirdly, everyone last night (except the female moderator) was surprised when I wanted to talk about the similarity between the guys in the novel and the guys who were concurrently waving their AR15s around in front of a dozen capitol buildings across the land, even though the reading series was called *On America*. The same men who, when I wear a mask into the grocery store, ask me if I am a snowflake. The same men who leer at Ruby and all the girls we love. We have tied ourselves into so many knots to have compassion, understanding, empathy for those guys, *The New York Times* alone has devoted thousands of column inches to them, and continues to. When have they ever, ever, once in their lives, tried to have compassion for us?

We are coming, I am sure of it, to either the end of the *letting men be in charge of the world* period of history, or the end of the human race. This pandemic must be the *something's got to give* moment. The men have failed the Earth and all her inhabitants dramatically, because of the weird insecurity absolute power imbues. We need look no further than the monster-in-chief to see it exaggerated so comically (if only we could laugh), no one who is not alive in this time would or will believe it is possible.

Because I am one of the few non-Native people who teach at IAIA, some students and faculty wish I were not there. Many more of them respect me, like me, are eager to work with me, a few even befriend me for real. But not one of them will ever fully trust me, because I am white (I know this is a questionable designation) and white people have been breaking promises and killing their relatives for centuries. *Five hundred years of genocide* is the constant refrain there, the de facto explanation for everything. Understanding, accepting, and working from within that truth has been one of the single most important educations of my life.

It has also given me a way to understand my current feelings about men, especially straight white men. I recognize there are good ones. I enjoy my time with many of them. I truly love a few of them. But I will never exactly trust them. Not entirely, not anymore. Not even the one I am married to, who is the best straight white man I have ever known.

Yesterday I asked Mike what he would do if a bunch of the men who threaten me on social media came up the driveway to kill me and the first thing he said was, "Make myself scarce."

It was an astonishing moment in our relationship, because what I had always pictured was him going out and talking to them calmly, because of his deep belief that they are good people, his Taoist commitment to the middle way. In my fantasy version of this event, I imagine them forgetting, in pretty short order, why they had come up the driveway in the first place. They would forget me entirely, and start talking about the elk they bagged last fall, or what a rip-off it is that the Forest Service charges ten dollars per cord of firewood.

Making Mike the enemy is even stupider than doing the same to Joe Wilkins. In the first place, what kind of feminist am I, if what I was looking for was to be saved from the marauders by my man? More to the point, Mike is good, and fair and loving and willing and eager to work hard emotionally in ways almost no one in my life experience, man or woman, has been. In all of those things he is more than my equal and I feel lucky to have found him every day. But when his first reaction was "make myself scarce," it made that distrusting pilot light flare up inside me, and even when he immediately shifted to "go out and confront them," I couldn't snuff it out.

What I wanted was not so much for Mike to tell me he would blow their heads off (a sentence Mike would never in this lifetime say) but to acknowledge my fear, and the possibility that in this red red part of Colorado my scenario is not entirely far-fetched. I'm pretty good with a gun too, though that scenario usually ends in multiple deaths whereas my driveway fantasy only ends in erasure. These are our choices, under this regime, and maybe the ones that came before. Every time I post or publish something political, I invite those guys to my driveway. And yet I keep posting, which must mean I believe erasure is worse.

One thing the pandemic has made crystal clear is exactly how much we are on our own. There is no safety net in this country of any kind, not for women, nor artists, nor educators, nor several of the other things I am. But there's a certain freedom in that, if a twisted one, bigger freedom in being willing to choose death over erasure, which is how so many Black/Latinx/Native/Asain artists and activists have lived and continue to live.

I would love living in a country that had my back, but since I don't, I feel under no obligation to please anybody. Not the government, nor the patriarchy, nor the publishing industry, nor *The New York Times*, nor even Mike, if it's at the expense of my own truth. I want to breathe. I want the next generation to be able to breathe. And to not be raped. And to not be shot. I want to love Mike, my friends, animals, and surrogate family members in a way that is bigger than pleasing. And I want to keep writing these letters.

Because the biggest dirty secret of all, one that decades (centuries) of gaslighting has made it possible for us to keep from ourselves is this: women

145

have more power in our little fingers than Mitch McConnell has in his entire ball sack. If he even has a ball sack. Mike Pence didn't need to wear a mask at the Mayo Clinic because he is actually made out of particle board and therefore doesn't have any lungs. I know fifty women personally who could set themselves on fire and fly to the moon if that's what they most wanted. It is the one thing I am most sure about, the largely untapped power of women. The administration is sure about it too. That's why they spend so much energy trying to keep us down.

Men have abdicated the right to control our lives, our air, and our water by a combination of incompetence, corruption, greed, and above all, insecurity.

Don't fucking tell me where the North Star is, asshole. Give me the sextant for a minute, and see how much better things get.

In love and rage,
Pam

PS A friend of mine who lives in the south received an email from their neighborhood online forum that said this:

Please, Mr. Mayor, give permission for the city beauty parlors to open for our lovely Wives,

Mothers, Daughters, Sisters to secure their scheduled treatments. Those chairs are appropriately separated. And it will do wonders for the men in their lives.

Below the email was a response, from a woman, one word, *amen*, with three praying hands emojis.

Dearest Pam,

It's Day 51 since we closed our front door to the outer world. It's also May Day—which the naked, naughty pagans, who were tortured and killed for loving the natural world, called Beltane. It is also almost Mother's Day, and as I mentioned, my mother sent lavender plants. In anticipation of their arrival, Devin and I drove to the nearest garden store, two river valleys away, for a nice blue pot and good soil, among other things. The marquis out front was inviting and said masks were required. (By the way, we finally got our antibody test results. All three of us were negative, although now there's talk that either the testing's not reliable, or antibodies don't mean squat, so who knows.)

Like you Pam, I live in a red corner of Colorado—a place where folks post "Trump 2020" yard signs but there are a few "Trump Jr 2024" signs, too. Like you, there is some eye-rolling when we cover our faces at the market or post office, but for the most part, folks in our town are leaving everyone to their own choices. But the garden store staff—masked and gloved, and still so accessible and helpful—suffered worse. As we paid up and said thanks, one employee, with tears in her eyes, said, "Thank you for helping us stay healthy. And thank you for not verbally assaulting us. Someone comes in every twenty minutes or so and just screams at us, calls us names, says that because of the mask requirement, they'll never shop here again. We are just trying to stay healthy, so we can keep our jobs, feed our families."

"Mayday" is the call for ships and airplanes in distress. It derives from the French phrase *m'aidez*, or "help me." *Aidez nous* is the plural form (you probably know that). I worry about our own protests, in these letters. There will be counter-protests—which is fine, that's what democracy's about. Until the men with guns march up the driveway. That's the antithesis of democracy. I can barely breathe, trying to imagine how this ends. Enough of this country believes that storming a state capitol with assault weapons, carrying signs that say let the sick die so the economy might live, is American.

Perhaps one reason that Barr's threat to punish the governors who have issued stricter stay-at-home orders most slays you is his departure from conservatives' firm belief in states' rights. How is it that Republicans are willing to forsake this cornerstone of their platform? If they don't hold the line on this one, if they can't see the delicate dance that values life as well as the dollar—if they can't see that this is no either-or situation—then our beloved democracy is dead in the water. I'm all for protest, for dissent, but this angry, weaponized defiance has nothing to do with tea getting tossed in the Boston Harbor.

I dreamed last night that an ex had his hands around my throat—a man who in the waking world had done the same. I couldn't speak. I couldn't breathe. I woke thinking, "They are gunning for a persistent chokehold." Depress our oxygen levels so we aren't clearheaded enough to locate the North Star when it's hanging there in the inkwell of night sky, dazzling as ever. So we can't take in air enough to walk toward it for as many miles as it takes, to arrive in a healthier, kinder world.

Like you, I am most afraid of living a life in which I cannot tell my story. I am most unwilling to live at the expense of less fortunate others—be they humans, Steller's jays, junipers.

I see clearly now, where to go. But I have been so lost. Every time, it's because I ignored my instincts and desires and followed some guy into his narrative: There's the boyfriend I took the heat for when he rear-ended another car and, since his drivers' license was suspended, begged me to switch seats before the cops got there. The boyfriend who told a teenage me to smoke "something cool," which I did, without question, only to learn later that it was crack cocaine. There's the therapist who told me to stop writing, because he thought I was "like Listerine," too blistering, too angry. It's inconceivable to me now that I obeyed.

I own my part here. But what staggers is how many men have put me in jeopardy, have used me as a rung on a ladder to get to high ground, and did so without ever asking how I felt about it. I'm not sure that any of them noticed—after all, it's marbled into cells, psyches, society. Just as it's ingrained for women who grow up with a father who pats your fifteen-year-old ass and tells you that the most important class you'll take in high school is typing—not so you can write books, but so you can get a good secretarial job. But only, he adds, if you keep the weight off those thunderous skier thighs.

There are bad guys out there who will read this and say terrible things about us. There will be threats, dismissals, or worse. Certainly there will be those who won't consider this real writing. But even a lot of the good guys out there will read this and bristle, push back, and dismiss the fact that sexism is a condition of maleness just as racism is a condition of whiteness—something we should be looking out for, apologizing for, and making amends for the rest of our lives. Those with the wealth and entitlement inherited from forefathers who built fortunes using enslaved Black people, who acquired land by killing the Native people, turned around and built the factory farms, the ski and golf resorts, the Amazon warehouses, the coal-fired power plants, the hunting safaris, the gated communities. But they also founded the environmental movement, and in the process they defended an idea of wilderness romanticized and chauvinized by John Wayne, Cormac McCarthy, and Edward Abbey. And until we come clean about that, until my liberal environmentalist friends stop trying to take me down at the Thanksgiving table by telling me that the story I want to write is irrelevant, uninteresting, and incapable of changing the world, their hands also grip our throats.

Last night I reread *Cowboys Are My Weakness*. It is such a sabre, slicing through the story that all is well between women and men, that we are enlightened enough to meet one another in bed, in the wilderness, in the halls of Congress, in a dark alleyway, or in the driveway, on equal ground. Sadly it's as relevant several decades later. Now I see why I first threw the book against the wall—because I envied that at that young age you had enough of yourself to push back against the lone white male narrative. During those years, I was leading hard climbs, running rescues, and guiding my squad out of wildfires that had turned on us, but I was lost in a story that wasn't my story. It would be several decades before I found my own. And then, when I finally told it, the backlash was swift and severe.

That's okay. It's better than living my life trapped in someone else's narrative, a narrative that requires that I either die by a man or be saved by a man. No, I only want a life in which I find my own way, before I die wizened and worn-out from a life that nearly burst at the end, so full it was with opportunities to speak, ride, dance, wander, teach, learn, love.

When Ruby was young, I stole away for a ski on the mountain that presides over our mesa—just the dogs and me. I meant to follow a large, open draw but a herd of mostly pregnant elk cows had bedded down in my path. I skirted them by plunging into thick timber. While I was in the forest, the sky clouded. The wind picked up and covered my tracks and I got totally turned around. It grew late, and there wasn't a landmark to aim for—not even the slant of the sun. The dogs paced in circles, staring at me, expectant. I wished then for a guy—father, spouse, bishop, therapist—to show me the way out. The wish was a fleeting one—a kind of flash fiction, and an insane one—because what else do you call it when you hand over your agency, your fate, to another person?

Men may not ask for directions (and that is another way I've been lost with them), but this is when I looked at Pablo and Ursa, my two crazy cow dogs, and said, "Go load up!" They spun around and headed off in the last direction I would have chosen, but I skied after them knowing they would obey my command to head for the car and launch themselves through the open hatchback. It was a race in the twilight, but sure enough, we found the vehicle.

In dreams, there are not only monsters who want to strangle you, there are dogs who listen when you speak. Jung called them psychopomps— beings that, if you are lost and ask for help, will lead you to God.

Dogs listen in the woods, too. And they'll lead you to safety every time. If home proves to be a place you cannot breathe, the dogs will follow you when you leave that story. So will those velvety herds of elk cows, and the forests—the elders and saplings and every tree in between.

If the guns come for us, Pam, grab your pen and notebook, your bivy sack, your flint and steel. Climb above tree line, on your side of the Great

Divide—which is the only thing that should separate our nation during this pandemic. Hell, even if they don't come, head up anyway. I'll meet you there with compass, envelopes, string. We won't go alone. We'll have the dogs. We'll have mentors, students, daughters. We'll have a few good men who are willing to walk with us, willing perhaps, to play supporting characters for a while, in the stories that need telling. And we'll have every other good creature, flanking us on all sides.

Let's bring our ballots, too. Let's fill them out and tie them to the tails of ravens passing through. Let's climb the ridgelines with the letters we have written and cast them into the clear blue sky. Then let's toss that compass into some deep icy ravine that never sees the light of day because already we know exactly where we're headed.

In fierce and loving sisterhood,
Amy

PS You have proved to be another one of my favorite animals—and we've yet to meet in person.

Dear Amy,

Your letter made me think of one of my favorite short stories, Ursula Le Guin's "Sur." I wonder if you know it. The story, published in 1982, set in 1909, chronicles a successful all-women expedition to the South Pole, during which, among other things, one of the explorers delivers a baby. The story stays with me because after the women overcome every hardship to finally reach the pole on December 22, 1909, and discuss leaving some kind of "mark or monument, a snow cairn, a tent pole or flag," they decide against it because "there seemed no particular reason to do so," because anything they were was "insignificant" in the face of that great landscape.

As they get ready to leave the Pole and head back to basecamp, one woman asks, "which way," and another answers, "north." The narrator tells us she is glad they are leaving no marker, "for some man longing to be the first might come some day and find it, and know then what a fool he had been, and break his heart."

I love this passage, not only because it explains my whole life to me, in the world of wilderness guiding, in the world of publishing, but also for the humor in that one-word answer. If there was an all-women expedition that got to the South Pole before Amundsen's team (and this is the magic of Le Guin, the way she adds the Sur Expedition to the annals of an alternate history), I bet they laughed a lot along the way.

What I always used to say about my years as a river and hunting and backpacking guide was this: "I never wanted to be better than the men at the outdoors, I just wanted to be good enough that they would invite me along, good enough that I could keep up. Ideally," I'd continue, "they would forget I was even there."

I'm not sure what to even say about this now, given all our letters have covered.

Way back in graduate school, in the heyday of deconstruction, I wrote a paper on Jacques Lacan's assertion that women, by virtue of not having a dick (or phallus, as he would have said), understand, far better than men, the truth of nonpossession. The man who taught the class told me, during office hours, I wasn't smart enough to write that paper, proving, more or less, Lacan's point. I went ahead and wrote the paper and got an A, a thing that professor was famous for not giving.

The same man, after *Cowboys Are My Weakness* came out, told me I was "glorifying an archaic form of masculinity." I noted, internally only, he was an archaic form of masculinity himself.

"Sur" is a story that is precisely about women understanding the truth of nonpossession. The environmental movement, in its purest and most effective form, must be about the same.

One more thing about me: when things are going relatively well in the world and in my life, I can fall down a disaster wormhole like nobody's business. But when the shit hits the fan for real, what I realize I cannot live without is hope.

Last night, as I worked on this letter, a video was leaked of the two white men who hunted down a young black jogger (Ahmaud Arbery) in a suburban neighborhood and killed him in cold blood, two men, who as of this writing, have faced no consequences for their actions. Even as I write these words, the current administration is trying, in the middle of this pandemic, to take health care away from millions. Yesterday the president called another female reporter a dog, and meant it as an insult! (As if…) Last night he called George Conway, whose mother is Filipino, Moonface, called the men with AR15s strapped to them breathing their COVID breaths onto security guards *very good people.*

"Your silence will not protect you," Audre Lorde says from the front of a T-shirt I have worn until it is threadbare, when I am not wearing the other one with a quote from Lidia Yuknavitch: "I am not the story you made of me."

Two days after my mother gave birth to me by caesarian, she wanted to go to a party. She was still in the hospital, but a little invasive surgery never kept my mother from a good time. She wheeled herself down to the maternity ward bulletin board and got Martha Washington's name off the list dedicated to newborn babysitting. Martha came to the hospital and watched me that night, miraculously fell in love with me, and didn't really leave until she died when I was twenty.

Martha taught me to swim, read, ride a bike, to hold open doors for my elders. She taught me generosity is its own reward, always, and that the failure of imagination has caused a scourge upon the Earth. Most importantly, she taught me to always, always, say yes to the world.

This morning on the dog walk I realized the thing I am afraid of far more than I am afraid of dying a breathless COVID death, far more than being shot in the face by a camo-wearing MAGA dude, is becoming a person who says no to the world. Becoming a person who doesn't go out, or hike out, or speak out, because prudence and my survival instinct tells me I should not. That would be the bad guys winning. That would be the bad guys winning most of all.

I can't say yes right now to a trek in Bhutan, or teaching a Writing in the Wild World class on a raft trip down the Dolores, or a march to protect women's access to contraception. But I can say yes to the tiny mountain ball cactus blooming near my clothesline. I can say yes to Lime Creek running over its banks (too early, too quickly) but braiding itself elegantly and generously quenching my pasture. I can say yes to my students, who I only see via Zoom these days, but who are still writing their stories like their lives depend on it, because if we don't know by now they do, we are definitely not paying attention. I can say yes to a horse named Ben, a thoroughbred/paint cross, a big boy, 16-3 and broad as a boat, dark bay with a shoulder that looks like someone threw a bucket of white paint at it. Ben needs a new home and I need something to say yes to, so he will arrive on the first of June. I can say yes to these letters, which are sustaining beyond all reason, except the reason we keep sending them across these mountains, these mountains that belong to everybody, and nobody, and mostly to themselves.

This administration can take so many things away from us. Our safety, our health care, our independence, our contraceptives, our freedom of movement, our livelihoods, our clean air and water, and inevitably, probably sooner than later, our right to speak. But it cannot keep us from saying yes to the world.

Whether this pandemic lasts for one year or three or a decade, we will emerge knowing far better what we need to survive. Even now, I can see the pencil scratching through item after item: airplane travel, hipster coffee, Wilco concert, baseball. What remains: air, water, horses, elk cows, ravens, and dogs. I have always put my faith in the concrete nouns of the world, but realize this list will have to include abstractions: community, trust, direct action, urgency, courage, sacrifice, love.

We have not one single thing to lose by believing, even now, that we can build the world we want to live in, and we must, because time is short and inaction is death. Fighting for the Earth and each other will be the only way to feel how alive we still are.

So let's save the post office. Let's win the election. Let's win *all* the elections. Let's downshift and tap into the power I know you know we have, the strength we feel when we put our feet on hard dirt, or words on these pages. Let's tend to the weary, the grieving, the hungry, to all those the system is rigged against. The Earth is our ally. She always has been. She understands the truth of nonpossession. In fact, she wrote the book on it.

Thank you for these letters, Amy. I hope there will be a thousand more. I will walk, now, to the back of my property, where the wetland is overflowing, breathe the clean air, and wait with a piece of string and this letter. Here I am now, my eyes trained on the ridgeline to the west.

In everlasting sisterhood.
Pam

ACKNOWLEDGMENTS:

These letters happened because *Orion* Magazine's visionary editor, Sumanth Prabhaker, invited us to correspond with each other for *Orion*'s online pandemic series, "Together Apart: Letters from Isolation." Once the *Orion* staff had so beautifully published our initial back-and-forth, we kept writing—and when the letters began to act like a larger work, we said as much to the intrepid women at Torrey House Press—Kirsten Johanna Allen, Kathleen Metcalf, Anne Terashima, Rachel Buck-Cockayne, and Michelle Wentling—who said *YES* to every word. Claire Taylor, who dwells exquisitely in all things animal, summoned the cover ravens, the belted kingfisher, the Steller's jay.

Standing with us are the men we love with every chamber in our hearts: our husbands, Devin Vaughan and Mike Blakeman. And our brother-in-arms who always knew we'd be friends, even before we penned the first letter, Craig Childs.

There are so many brave and bighearted people on the front lines who not only deserve plenty of PPE, but also hazard pay, months-long vacations, and to have their mortgages paid in full—retroactive to February when they first risked their lives that we might keep breathing and eating. We are especially grateful to the postmistresses who run each of our small-town post offices (LONG LIVE THE UNITED STATES POST OFFICE!), and our UPS drivers—who are both women and the only delivery people unfazed by our overzealous dogs. They are also the only delivery people who can, after a big storm, make a three-point turn in our driveways without getting stuck.

If this book is anything, it is tribute to the young women who are fighting for the Earth, the animals, the vulnerable humans—Emma González, Isra Hirsi, Mari Copeny, Sophie Cruz, Greta Thunberg, Nadya Okamoto, Helena Gualinga, Jamie Margolin, Autumn Peltier, Artemisa Xakriabá, Leah Namugerwa, Charitie Ropati, Naelyn Pike, Jessica Smith. And Ruby, who's ridden the warhorses since birth.

Then there's Earth. May she thrive again.

ABOUT THE AUTHORS

PAM HOUSTON is the author of the memoir, *Deep Creek: Finding Hope In The High Country*, as well as two novels, *Contents May Have Shifted* and *Sight Hound*, two collections of short stories, *Cowboys Are My Weakness* and *Waltzing the Cat*, and a collection of essays, *A Little More About Me*, all published by W.W. Norton. She teaches in the Low Rez MFA program at the Institute of American Indian Arts, is Professor of English at UC Davis, and cofounder and creative director of the literary nonprofit Writing By Writers. She lives at nine thousand feet above sea level near the headwaters of the Rio Grande.

AMY IRVINE is a sixth-generation Utahn and longtime public lands activist. She is the author of *Desert Cabal: A New Season in the Wilderness*. Her memoir, *Trespass: Living at the Edge of the Promised Land*, received the Orion Book Award, the Ellen Meloy Desert Writers Award, and the Colorado Book Award. Irvine teaches in the Mountainview MFA program of Southern New Hampshire University. She lives and writes in southwest Colorado, just spitting distance from her Utah homeland.

ABOUT THE ART

The cover image, interior Stellar's jay sketch, and interior belted kingfisher sketch were all created for this book by Claire Taylor.

Find her work at www.clairetaylor.art.

TORREY HOUSE PRESS

Voices for the Land

The economy is a wholly owned subsidiary of the environment, not the other way around.

—Senator Gaylord Nelson, founder of Earth Day

Torrey House Press publishes books at the intersection of the literary arts and environmental advocacy. THP authors explore the diversity of human experiences with the environment and engage community in conversations about landscape, literature, and the future of our ever-changing planet, inspiring action toward a more just world. We believe that lively, contemporary literature is at the cutting edge of social change. We seek to inform, expand, and reshape the dialogue on environmental justice and stewardship for the human and more-than-human world by elevating literary excellence from diverse voices.

Visit www.torreyhouse.org for reading group discussion guides, author interviews, and more.

As a 501(c)(3) nonprofit publisher, our work is made possible by generous donations from readers like you.

This book was made possible by generous gifts from Elaine Deschamps, Lindsey Leavell, James and Wendie Highsmith, Laurie Galbreath, Helen Pyne, the LARRK Foundation, the Ruth H. Brown Foundation, and the Sam & Diane Stewart Family Foundation. Torrey House Press is supported by Back of Beyond Books, the King's English Bookshop, Jeff and Heather Adams, the Jeffrey S. and Helen H. Cardon Foundation, Diana Allison, Jerome Cooney and Laura Storjohann, Robert Aagard and Camille Bailey Aagard, Heidi Dexter and David Gens, Kirtly Parker Jones, the Utah Division of Arts & Museums, the National Endowment for the Humanities, the National Endowment for the Arts, and Salt Lake County Zoo, Arts & Parks. Our thanks to individual donors, subscribers, and the Torrey House Press board of directors for their valued support.

Join the Torrey House Press family and give today at www.torreyhouse.org/give.